Edinburgh Law Essentials

# DELICT ESSENTIALS

D0257348

# EDINBURGH LAW ESSENTIALS

*Series Editor*: Nicholas Grier, Edinburgh Napier Universi

*Private International Law*
David Hill

*Revenue Law Essentials*
William Craig

*Commercial Law Essentials*
Malcolm Combe

*Succession Law Essentials*
Frankie McCarthy

*Delict Essentials*
Francis McManus

*Scottish Legal System Essentials*
Bryan Clark and Gerard Keegan

*Scottish Evidence Law Essentials*
James Chalmers

*Contract Law Essential Cases*
Tikus Little

*Trusts Law Essentials*
John Finlay

*Company Law Essentials*
Josephine Bisacre and Claire McFadzean

*Jurisprudence Essentials*
Duncan Spiers

*Legal Method Essentials for Scots Law*
Dale McFadzean and Lynn Allardyce Irvine

*Human Rights Law Essentials*
Valerie Finch and John McGroarty

*Planning Law Essentials*
Anne-Michelle Slater

*Scottish Contract Law Essentials*
Tikus Little

*Employment Law Essentials*
Jenifer Ross

*International Law Essentials*
John Grant

*Media Law Essentials*
Douglas Maule and Zhongdong Niu

*Intellectual Property Law Essentials*
Duncan Spiers

*Scottish Family Law*
Kenneth Norrie

*European Law Essentials*
Stephanie Switzer

*Roman Law Essentials*
Craig Anderson

*Property Law Essentials*
Duncan Spiers

*Medical Law Essentials*
Murray Earle

*Public Law Essentials*
Jean McFadden and Dale McFadzean

*Scottish Administrative Law Essentials*
Jean McFadden and Dale McFadzean

www.edinburghuniversitypress.com/series/ele

Edinburgh Law Essentials

# DELICT ESSENTIALS

## Third edition

Francis McManus, M.Litt., LL.B. (Hons),
F.R.I.P.H., F.H.E.A., M.R.E.H.I.S., Cert. Ed.

*Honorary Professor of Law, University of
Stirling and Emeritus Professor of Law,
Edinburgh Napier University*

EDINBURGH
University Press

Edinburgh University Press is one of the leading university presses in the UK. We publish academic books and journals in our selected subject areas across the humanities and social sciences, combining cutting-edge scholarship with high editorial and production values to produce academic works of lasting importance. For more information visit our website: edinburghuniversitypress.com

Previous editions published in 2008 and 2013 by Dundee University Press

Edinburgh University Press Ltd
The Tun – Holyrood Road
12 (2f) Jackson's Entry
Edinburgh EH8 8PJ

Typeset in Bembo by
IDSUK (DataConnection) Ltd, and
printed and bound in Great Britain by
CPI Group (UK) Ltd, Croydon CR0 4YY

A CIP record for this book is available from the British Library

ISBN 978 1 4744 1750 1 (paperback)
ISBN 978 1 4744 1751 8 (webready PDF)
ISBN 978 1 4744 1752 5 (epub)

# CONTENTS

*In memory of my parents*

# TABLE OF CASES

# TABLE OF STATUTES

# 1 INTRODUCTION

The law of delict is concerned with civil wrongs, that is to say the law which governs compensation or reparation for damage which one individual inflicts upon another. The law imposes upon the person who injures another an obligation to compensate that person. The obligation which is thus imposed arises *ex lege* (by law), in contrast to that which arises *ex contractu* (by way of contract).

The law imposes a unilateral obligation on the person who commits a wrongful act to compensate the person who is injured. Such injury or harm may take a number of forms. It may take the form of injury which is caused to one's person, for example that caused by a road accident or an accident at work. However, the injury or damage which is the subject-matter of an action in delict may take quite different forms. I might sustain financial loss because I have relied on negligent advice which was given to me by my financial adviser who suggested that I should invest money in a newly floated company which soon goes into liquidation. However, the harm in question may take more subtle forms. For example, it could consist of the loss of my reputation or of hurt feelings as a result of what has been written about me. The law of defamation allows me to recover for such injury in certain circumstances. Again, the injury could comprise my being annoyed by my neighbour's constant guitar playing. The law of nuisance can provide a remedy in such circumstances.

However, not every human act which causes injury or harm allows one to be compensated in the law of delict. For example, a petrol station may be put out of business soon after a large supermarket petrol station commences operation in the vicinity. The proprietor of the former would have no remedy in the law of delict since, in the eye of the law, the owners of the supermarket have done no wrong.

There are a number of theories as to the function and role of the law of delict. The respective theories overlap. Occasionally, judges refer to such theories in their judgments. However, in the majority of cases, they do not.

Some argue that the law of delict operates to control the behaviour of people before they perform a particular act which has the potential to cause harm. I, therefore, refrain from consuming alcohol before I set out on a car journey because I know that if I injure a fellow road user I could be sued. I refrain from assaulting you for the same reason. However, one could argue that in such cases it is not the fear that I may be required to compensate my victim which prompts me to act in a non-delictual way, but, rather, fear of my incurring sanction under the criminal law: I might be sent to jail for drunk-driving or assaulting you! One could also argue that another reason for my refraining from acting in a delictual way is not fear of any form of legal sanction, whether civil or criminal, but rather fear of public opprobrium. The public, generally speaking, think less of people who act in such a manner.

Another function of the law of delict is based on distributive justice. This principle is founded on the premise that by spreading the loss from an individual victim to those who benefit from an activity, the loss is more easily borne in terms of society as a whole. For example, a public utility which is forced to compensate someone who is injured in a gas explosion, is able to absorb the cost by raising the price of its service among those who benefit from it, namely the public. Another example of the principle of distributive justice is seen in the concept of vicarious liability. Here, an employer (who can more easily bear the legal obligation to compensate the victim than his employee) is held strictly liable (that is to say, liable without fault) for the delicts of his employees. The same principle applies to a situation in which a defective product injures a consumer. The producer can spread his loss (represented in terms of his obligation to compensate the victim) by raising the price of his products.

However, some are of the view that the requirements of distributive justice can also be satisfied simply by allowing the loss to lie where it falls. For example, in *McFarlane* v *Tayside Health Board* (2000) the pursuers were negligently advised that a vasectomy had rendered the husband infertile. The couple relied on that advice and ceased to take contraceptive precautions. A child was subsequently born to them. The couple sued the health board for the financial loss which they would incur in bringing up the child. However, the House of Lords rejected their claim. Lord Steyn was of the view (at 82) that such losses were those which society (some of whom wanted but could not have children, others who had to bring up disabled children) as a whole, had to bear. It would not be morally acceptable for the law to transfer to the health board the loss in respect of which the pursuer claimed compensation.

The main function of the law of delict is to compensate the victim for the damage or injury which he has sustained, whether such damage sounds in terms of economic loss or physical injury.

The law of delict, unlike, for example, the law of evidence or the law of succession, consists of a number of separate delicts. Indeed, there is no logical reason why this book could not have been entitled *Delicts*. Some delicts, such as assault, comprise intentional acts on the part of the defender, whereas other delicts, such as negligence, do not. Furthermore, in some delicts, such as nuisance and defamation, there also exist elements of intention and negligence. For example, I may intend to publish a defamatory statement about a particular person but not about the defender of whose existence I should have known.

There are thus a variety of delicts which are recognised by law. This book simply covers those which are considered to be the more important.

# 2  NEGLIGENCE

The vast majority of civil actions which are brought before the courts concern negligence. Negligent conduct can take many forms. It can consist of accidents which occur at work by virtue of an employer's negligence. The negligent conduct could also comprise negligent driving on the roads, or the giving of negligent advice by a financial adviser to a client.

What we must examine is how the courts have attempted to ascertain whether liability exists for harm which is caused by various forms of negligent conduct. We will see that, for policy reasons, the courts are more willing to allow a negligence claim to succeed for certain types of injury than for others.

In order to recover for damage which is caused by negligent conduct, the pursuer requires to prove that:

(1) the defender owes the pursuer a *duty of care* in law;

(2) the *standard of care* which the law demands of the defender has been breached; and

(3) the negligent act in question *caused* the requisite injury to the pursuer.

## (1) DUTY OF CARE

In order to ascertain whether the defender is liable in law for the damage which he has caused, the court must decide whether the defender owed the pursuer a duty of care in law.

During the 19th century, with the advent of road and rail transport and, indeed, industrialisation in general, negligence actions were increasingly being brought before the courts. By the end of the century the courts had already established that a doctor owed a duty of care to a patient in respect of the treatment which was given to the patient; a road user owed a duty of care to another in respect of the former's conduct on the road; and an occupier of land, in certain circumstances, owed a duty of care to those who visited the land. However, the courts had never really worked out a general formula whereby one could establish whether the defender owed a duty of care to the pursuer in a novel situation, that is to say a situation or circumstances which had not previously been decided by the courts.

There had been several attempts by judges to work out such a formula. However, the real breakthrough came with the landmark decision of the House of Lords in *Donoghue* v *Stevenson* (1932). In that case Mrs Donoghue went into a café in Paisley. Her friend brought her an ice cream and a ginger beer. The ginger beer had been manufactured by Stevenson. The café proprietor poured some of the ginger beer into Mrs Donoghue's glass and she consumed some of the contents. Her friend then poured the remainder of the ginger beer into her glass. As he did so, the remains of a decomposed snail floated out of the bottle. Mrs Donoghue claimed that she suffered nervous shock and gastro-enteritis as a consequence. Of course, Mrs Donoghue did not have a contract with Stevenson, since her friend had bought the ginger beer from the café proprietor. Therefore, in order to succeed, she had to sue Stevenson in the law of delict. The question which the court had to answer was whether the manufacturer of the beer, Stevenson, owed a duty of care to Mrs Donoghue as the consumer. The House of Lords held that a duty of care was owed by the former to the latter. Lord Atkin stated:

> "The rule that you are to love your neighbour becomes in law, you must not injure your neighbour … You must take reasonable care to avoid acts or omissions which would be likely to injure your neighbour. Who then is my neighbour? … persons who are so closely affected by my act that I ought reasonably to have them in contemplation as being so affected when I am directing my mind to the acts or omissions which are called into question."

In other words, according to Lord Atkin, if one could reasonably foresee that one's conduct could harm the pursuer, a duty of care would arise.

A good example of the application of the Atkinian foreseeability can be seen in *Beaumont* v *Surrey County Council* (1968). Here, a teacher discarded a long piece of elastic in an open bin. The elastic was used in horseplay between pupils and the claimant lost an eye. The education authority was held liable since it was foreseeable that such an accident would take place. The foreseeability principle was applied again in the House of Lords case of *Home Office* v *Dorset Yacht Company* (1970). In that case a party of Borstal trainees were working on Brownsea Island in Poole Harbour, under the supervision and control of three Borstal officers. During the night, seven of the trainees escaped and went aboard a yacht which was anchored nearby. The boys could not navigate properly, which resulted in a collision and damage to a yacht owned by the Dorset Yacht Company which successfully sued the Home Office in negligence. Essentially, the House of Lords held that the defendant owed a duty of care to the claimants because such an occurrence was foreseeable. Lord Reid stated: "the time has come when we can and should say that (Lord Atkin's neighbour principle) ought to apply unless there is some justification or valid explanation for excluding liability in negligence".

It can be seen that Lord Reid is suggesting that a duty of care should be held to exist if one can foresee that one's conduct will injure someone else. However, that duty of care would be negated if policy reasons dictated.

## Two-staged approach

Lord Reid's approach in *Dorset Yacht* really implied that one should take a two-staged approach in ascertaining whether a duty of care should lie between the defender and the pursuer. The scene was, therefore, set for the for the formal endorsement of such an approach in the House of Lords case of *Anns v Merton London Borough Council* (1977). In that case, a builder negligently constructed the foundations of a building which was being constructed and the walls began to crack. The lessees of the building sued the local authority (which was responsible for ensuring that the building works complied with the relevant building control legislation), in effect, for failing to protect them from incompetent builders. The House of Lords held that the local authority did owe the lessees a duty of care in law. Lord Wilberforce enunciated a two-staged approach to the duty of care. In his view, if the court were confronted with a novel situation (that is to say, one which had not come before the courts previously) one should approach the concept of duty of care in the following way:

(a) first, if a sufficient relationship of proximity exists between the parties then, *prima facie*, a duty of care arises; and

(b) second, if such a duty of care does arise, it is then necessary to consider whether there are any considerations which ought to negative, reduce or limit the scope of such duty.

In deciding if there was a sufficiently close relationship, one would still rely on the foreseeability test of Lord Atkin in *Donoghue v Stevenson* (1932). However, if one formed the view that a duty of care arose, one would ascertain if there were any policy grounds for excluding liability. We can see here that such an approach to the duty of care allows a court to extend the boundaries of the law of negligence fairly readily. A good example of the courts using the two-staged approach to expand the duty of care is seen in *McLoughlin v O'Brian* (1983). In that case the House of Lords had to consider whether a mother who sustained nervous shock by visiting, in hospital, her family who had been seriously injured by the negligence of the defendant could succeed in a negligence action. Prior to the case being decided it was necessary that a secondary victim of nervous shock had to witness the actual accident itself before he could succeed in a negligence claim. The House applied the two-staged approach to the duty of care to allow her to recover.

However, this expansive approach to the duty of care was relatively short lived. In *Governors of the Peabody Fund v Sir Lindsay Parkinson* (1985) the House of Lords had to consider whether a local authority was liable to building contractors for failing to ascertain at the time of inspection that the drains which were being installed on a building site were unsuitable. In holding that the local authority was not liable for the loss which was sustained, the House took into account not only whether there was sufficient proximity between the defendant and the plaintiff but also whether it would be fair, just and reasonable to impose a duty of care. Several years later, in *Yuen Kun-Yeu v Attorney-General of Hong Kong* (1987), individuals who had deposited money in a bank sued the Government, in effect, for failing to regulate a bank properly, resulting in their losing money. The Privy Council was of the view that the law should develop novel categories of negligence incrementally and by analogy, rather than by a massive extension of a *prima facie* duty of care which was restrained only by indefinable considerations which sought to negative, reduce or limit the scope of the duty or class of person to whom it is owed. In other words, the Privy Council advocated an approach in which more sanctity should be accorded to previously decided cases. If a novel factual set of circumstances were presented before the court it would ascertain whether the courts had decided a case which was analogous to the present facts. In any case, the law should allow the boundaries of the duty of care to be expanded gradually or incrementally.

Another decisive blow against the two-staged approach to the duty of care came with the decision in *Caparo v Dickman* (1990). In that case shareholders brought an action in negligence against auditors, on the ground that the latter had negligently prepared an audit, the consequences of which were that the shareholders had purchased shares in reliance on the relevant report and had suffered financial loss. The House of Lords held that no duty of care was owed by the auditors to the shareholders. A relationship of proximity or neighbourhood was required to exist between the plaintiffs and the defendants. The House also had to consider it fair, just and reasonable that the law should impose a duty of a given scope. Furthermore, foreseeability and proximity were different things. Foreseeability was a necessary but not a sufficient requirement to establish a duty of care in negligence.

An important question which fell to be answered in the wake of the incremental approach being instituted was whether, in determining whether a duty of care existed, one should adopt a similar approach to claims which pertain to physical harm as to those pertaining to economic loss. In *Marc Rich and Co* v *Bishop Rock Marine Ltd* (1996) a ship was negligently surveyed by the defendant. It was put to sea in reliance on the survey. However, the ship was damaged and soon sank, resulting in its loss and also that of the cargo. The House of Lords held that the law should not draw any distinction between the type of harm which the claimant sustains when ascertaining whether a duty of care lies. In other words, the application of the incremental approach was appropriate irrespective of the type of loss which was sustained.

The issue as to whether the tripartite test applies to personal injuries which have been sustained by the pursuer as a result of the defender's negligence was discussed in the Court of Appeal case of *Everett* v *Comojo (UK) Ltd t/a The Metropolitan* (2012). The facts of the case were simple. The claimants visited a nightclub. They were attacked and seriously injured by another guest. The claimants claimed that the club had failed to adopt appropriate measures to prevent the assault from taking place. The court held that the club owed the claimants a duty of care in terms of the law of negligence. The relationship between the management and its guests was of sufficient proximity to justify the existence of a duty of care by the defender to the pursuer. The management was in control of the premises. Furthermore, the management could regulate who entered the premises and also could regulate who was to be removed after entry. There was also an economic relationship between the two parties. Furthermore, given the relationship between the consumption of alcohol and violence, it was foreseeable that one guest might attack another. It was also fair, just and reasonable that a duty of care should be imposed in order to govern the relationship between the managers of a hotel or nightclub and their guests in relation to the actions of third parties. However, on the facts of the case the club had not breached its duty of care to the claimants.

Another interesting example of the application of the incremental approach to the duty of care can be seen in *Watson* v *British Boxing Board of Control* (2001). This case concerned head injuries sustained by Michael Watson, a professional boxer, in his title fight with Chris Eubank. The fight was regulated by the British Boxing Board of Control (BBBC). Watson claimed that the BBBC had failed to take adequate measures to ensure that he received immediate and effective medical attention should he sustain injury during the fight. The Court of Appeal held that there was sufficient proximity between the parties to ground a duty of care in law. Furthermore, since the BBBC had complete control over the contest it was fair, just and reasonable to conclude that a duty of care existed. In his judgment (at 1281) Lord Phillips set store by the following factors:

(1) Watson was one of a defined number of boxing members of the BBBC.

(2) A primary stated object of the BBBC was to look after its boxing members' physical safety.

(3) The BBBC encouraged and supported its boxing members in the pursuit of an activity which involved inevitable physical injury.

(4) The BBBC controlled the medical assistance which could be provided.

(5) The BBBC had access to specialist expertise in relation to medical care.

(6) If Watson had no remedy against the BBBC, he had no remedy at all.

(7) Boxing members of the BBBC, including Watson, could reasonably rely on the former to look after their safety.

Factor 1 neatly illustrates the disinclination of the courts to impose on a defender a duty of care to a potentially large number of people. We will see this approach illustrated again in relation to claims for pure economic loss, claims in respect of loss which is caused by negligent statements and claims in respect of psychiatric injury.

## The duty of care and public authorities

Thus far, we have looked at how the courts have addressed the extent, if any, to which private individuals owe a duty of care to each other in terms of the law of negligence. We now consider the extent to which public bodies, such as local authorities, owe such a duty to members of the public. However, unlike private individuals, public authorities are purely creatures of statute. That is to say, public authorities derive both their duties and powers solely from Acts of Parliament. The nature of such duties and powers is wide-ranging indeed and they extend from a relevant authority ensuring that buildings which are being constructed in its area are of sound construction, to its making provision for suitable education, social care and housing for the local community. This aspect of the law of negligence probably represents a particularly grey area of the law. We now look at how the courts have addressed the liability of public authorities in terms of separate functions or authorities, for example the police. However, this is done simply for the sake of convenience. The separate categories of functions or public authorities should not be regarded as either self contained, or watertight, in terms of the law of negligence.

## The police

The general rule is that the courts are unwilling to impose an affirmative duty on the police to prevent third parties from inflicting harm on the public. This principle is well illustrated in the House of Lords case of *Hill v Chief Constable of West Yorkshire* (1989). In that case, the mother of one of the Yorkshire Ripper's victims sued the Chief Constable of West Yorkshire for the failure on the part of the police to apprehend the Yorkshire Ripper as a result of which he murdered her daughter. The House held that whereas it was reasonably foreseeable that if the Ripper (Peter Sutcliffe) was not apprehended, he would inflict serious bodily harm on members of the public, no duty of care was owed by the police to his victim. There was no proximity between the police and the victim. Furthermore, it was against public policy to hold the police civilly liable for failure to apprehend a criminal. Essentially, if such a duty were to be imposed, this would result in a significant diversion of police manpower and attention from the police's most important function, that of the suppression of crime.

The learning in *Hill* was endorsed by the House of Lords in *Van Colle v Chief Constable of Hertfordshire Police* (2008). In that case, the essential question which fell to be answered by the House was simply: if the police are alerted to a threat that X may kill or inflict violence on V, and the police take no action to prevent that occurrence, and D does kill or inflict violence on V, may either V or his relatives obtain civil redress against the police and, if so, in which circumstances? Since *Hill* the Human Rights Act 1998 has incorporated the European Convention on Human Rights (ECHR) into domestic law. Article 2 of the Convention provides that "everyone's life shall be protected by law. No one shall be deprived of his life intentionally". Furthermore, in the ECHR case of *Osman v UK* (1998) the court held that the state would be liable only if it was established that the authorities either knew, or ought to have known, at the relevant time, of the existence of a real and immediate risk to the life of an individual by a third party and that the necessary measures were not taken. The fundamental question which the House had to consider was the extent, if any, to which the policy of the common law was required to be reconsidered in the light of such jurisprudence. The House decided that *Hill* was not undermined by *Osman*.

The learning in the above cases which concerned liability of the police for failing to protect the general public from harm which is inflicted by others was applied in the Outer House case of *Thomson* v *Scottish Ministers* (2011). In that case the pursuer was the mother of a woman, X, who had been murdered by Y. Y had been temporarily released from prison, during which time he murdered X. The pursuer claimed that the Scottish Prison were negligent in releasing Y from prison and also owed X a duty of care in terms of the law of negligence. However, Lord Brodie held that the action fell to be dismissed.

In the Court of Appeal case of *An Informer* v *A Chief Constable* (2012) the court was required to answer the novel question of whether a supplier of information (ie the informer, C) to the police which led to a criminal investigation was owed, *inter alia*, a duty of care by the police to exercise reasonable care in the conduct of the investigation so as to safeguard C from both psychiatric injury and also pure economic loss. In the instant case, C had supplied the police with information about the suspected criminal activity on the part of others. However, C had also become a suspect and was arrested. The police who were responsible for C's arrest had applied for and were granted a restraint order against C, specifying certain assets. The upshot of this was that the assets could not be sold. The judge who made the order was told nothing about C's role as an informer. Furthermore, neither the police officer who had made the statement in support of the application nor the Crown Prosecution Service had been informed of C's role. C claimed, *inter alia*, that by virtue of the relationship which C had with the police the latter had assumed a responsibility to C in respect of his welfare, livelihood and reputation. At first instance, as far as the claim in tort was concerned, (with the exception of the claim for psychiatric injury) the type of loss on which C founded his action ranked as pure economic loss. As far as the claim relating to psychiatric injury was concerned, the loss was not foreseeable. Therefore, the claim failed. C appealed in relation to the claim based on pure economic loss.

In the Court of Appeal Toulson LJ was of the view that the relationship between C and the police was a confidential relationship. The defendant owed a duty of care to protect C from risks to his physical safety to which he was exposed in his role as an informer. However, the duty did not extend to protecting C from investigation of suspected criminal conduct on his part. Nor did the duty extend to purely economic loss. In the view of Arden LJ there was an assumption of a duty of care on the part of the police to C in his capacity as an informer. However, in the last analysis, the assumption of responsibility which was imposed on the police was displaced by the investigations immunity which was enshrined in the *Hill* principle. For Pill LJ, a special relationship between the police and C did exist. However, his Lordship went on to hold that the failure of the police to notify the front-line investigators of C's status did not constitute a breach of the duty of care which was owed by the former to the latter.

The application of the so-called *Hill* principle, whereby the courts display a pronounced reluctance to impose a duty of care on the police for failing to prevent members of the public being harmed by criminals, was seen again in the Supreme Court case of *Michael v Chief Constable of South Wales Police* (2015). In that case, a female member of the public (the victim) made an emergency phone call from her mobile phone, to the police from her home. The call was received at a mast which was situated across the county border. Therefore, the call was taken by a call-handler from the neighbouring police force. The victim informed the call-handler that her ex-partner had visited her home, had found her with another man and had assaulted her. Later in the same phone call, the victim reported that her partner had threatened to return to her home and kill her. However, the call-handler apparently failed to hear her say that. The victim was advised that the call would be passed to the appropriate police force. The phone call was then graded as requiring an immediate response, envisaging the police visiting her house within five minutes. The call handler then contacted the control room of the appropriate police force. The police force were informed that the victim had claimed that she had been assaulted but were not informed that the victim had claimed that her ex-partner had threatened to return to her home in order to kill her. Accordingly, the call was graded as requiring lower priority and demanding a response within 60 minutes. Before the police responded to the original call the victim made another 999 call during which she was heard to scream. The police responded immediately. They found the victim, who had been stabbed to death. The claimants (the victim's estate and her dependents) then raised an action under common law negligence and under Art 2 of the ECHR (which guarantees the right to life) against both police forces.

As far as the claim in negligence was concerned, the Supreme Court held (by a majority) that the police did not owe an individual member of the public a duty of care in relation to the manner in which it performed its duty. Rather, the police owed a duty to preserve the peace only to the public at large, in contradistinction to individual members of the public.

We have seen that the courts are unwilling, on grounds of public policy, to impose a duty of care on the police for their failure to apprehend criminals who proceed to harm members of the public. However, to what extent, if any, is the learning in *Hill* applicable to a situation where a member of the police force is injured in the course of carrying out his duties? In short, does the unwillingness on the part of the courts to impose an affirmative duty of care on the police in the performance of their duties vis-à-vis the public, extend to the duty of care which a police authority owes to its constables? This issue fell to be decided in *Rathband* v *The Chief Constable of Northumbria Constabulary* (2016). In that case, Rathband, a police constable, was on duty. In the early hours of the previous day, one Raoul Moat had shot and injured his former partner and had killed his present partner. As a result of his extremely violent conduct, he was the subject of an extensive police manhunt. On the morning that Rathband was seriously injured by Moat, the latter had made a 999 call during which he had threatened to injure or kill police officers. He concluded by saying that he was, "hunting for officers now". Less than nine minutes later he shot, and seriously injured, Rathband. Rathband committed suicide in 2012. However, before he died, he had commenced proceedings against the Chief Constable, alleging that the police owed him a duty of care to immediately warn him of the threats which Moat had made. The action against the police was continued by his estate. At first instance, it was held that whereas a chief constable owes a duty of care to officers within his force to take reasonable care for their safety both by the provision and operation of a safe system of work, the Chief Constable's duty as a quasi-employer could be outweighed by public policy considerations, as represented in *Hill*. Furthermore, on the application of the *Caparo* tripartite test, it would not be fair, just and reasonable to impose a duty of care on the police. The claimants, therefore, failed in their action.

### Fire authorities, the ambulance service and the coastguard

The extent to which the fire service was under a duty to rescue was considered in *Duff* v *Highlands and Islands Fire Board* (1995). In that case the defenders had been called out to the house which adjoined that of the pursuer twice in one evening. On their first visit, the fire brigade left while the house was still on fire. The fire brigade was recalled. However, it was unable to put out the fire. The fire spread to the pursuer's premises, which were destroyed. It was claimed on behalf of the defender that it was contrary to public policy for the law to hold that a duty of care was owed to the pursuer, on the ground that this might tend to encourage a defensive approach to the performance of the fire-fighting duties of the defender. This argument was rejected in the Outer House. The defender was held liable in terms of the law of negligence.

However, a different approach to the imposition of a duty of care was taken in *Church of Jesus Christ of Latter-Day Saints (Great Britain)* v *Yorkshire Fire and Civil Defence Authority* (1996). In that case, a fire brigade failed to extinguish a fire at the claimant's premises because the defendant fire authority had failed to ensure that certain fire hydrants at the premises were in working order. However, it was held contrary to public policy to impose a duty of care in terms of the law of negligence, since the imposition of a duty of care would essentially distract the attention of fire-fighters from their primary responsibility of fighting fires. Again, in *John Munroe (Acrylics) Ltd* v *London Fire and Civil Defence Authority* (1996) a fire was caused by certain people on wasteland which was not far from the claimant's premises. Fire engines arrived in response to emergency calls, by which time the burning debris and also the fires on the waste ground had been extinguished and there was no evidence of any continuing fire. Believing that the fires had been extinguished and that the danger had passed, the fire crews left. Unfortunately, the fire crews had not inspected the claimant's premises which abutted on one side of the waste ground where there was combustible material. Fire damaged the premises. At first instance, it was held that the fire authority did not owe the claimant a duty of care at common law. There was insufficient proximity between the fire brigades and the owners of any property which was on fire to impose a duty of care on the former to the latter. Furthermore, it was contrary to public policy to impose a common-law duty of care on a fire authority for failing to extinguish a fire. There were a number of factors which made it contrary to public policy to impose such a duty:

(1) no extra standard of care would be achieved;

(2) common-law duty of care would lead to defensive firefighting;

(3) the efficiency of the emergency services should be tested but not in private litigation;

(4) the fire brigade acted for the collective welfare of the community;

(5) successful claims against any fire authority would require to be subscribed by the general public – it was preferable that the floodgates should remain closed to such claims.

The courts are more willing to impose liability in respect of liability in the performance of an operational duty, for example the closure of the approach to a bridge by the police (*Gibson* v *Orr* (1999)) since, for one thing, it is easier for the courts to ascertain whether the requisite standard of care has been breached. Again in *Duff* v *Highland and Islands Fire Board* (1995) a fire brigade attended a house chimney fire. The brigade left before the fire was properly extinguished. As a result, two houses were destroyed. In the Outer House Lord Macfadyen expressed the view that it was not contrary to public policy to impose a duty of care on the fire service towards the owners of the houses. *Duff* can be contrasted with *Capital and Counties plc* v *Hampshire CC* (1996). In that case the plaintiffs were tenants of a commercial building. A fire broke out in part of the building which was equipped with sprinkler system. The fire brigade attended the fire. The officer in charge ordered that the sprinkler system be shut down. The fire went out of control as a result of this action. The building was destroyed. The court held that the defendant fire service owed the claimants a duty of care in law. The very act of shutting down the sprinkler system generated a relationship of proximity between the defendants and the plaintiffs. Furthermore, there were no policy grounds for excluding liability on the part of the defendants. See also *Burnett* v *Grampian Fire and Rescue Service* (2007). However, the potential liability of the fire authorities for the negligent discharge of their fire-fighting duties requires to be reviewed in the light of the recent Inner House case of *A J Allan (Blairnyle) Ltd* v *Strathclyde Fire Board* (2016). Here, the defender a fire brigade was called to attend to a fire which had broken out in a farmhouse which was owned by the first pursuer and used by the second pursuer. Fire tenders arrived and extinguished the fire. They left at about 3 p.m. However, in the early hours of the morning the fire reignited. The pursuers alleged that this occurred as a result of smouldering rotten timbers in the roof space. The farmhouse burned down. The court, in deciding in favour of the defender, endorsed the approach which was taken by the House of Lords in *East Suffolk Rivers Catchment Board* v *Kent* (1941). In that case, the defendant board (which was acting under statutory powers) had failed to adequately repair a sea wall and effectively deal with subsequent flooding, the upshot of which was that the claimant's property was damaged. The House decided in favour of the defendant board on the basis that notwithstanding the fact that the defendant board had been negligent, in effect, it had not made matters worse. That is to say, that if the board had simply decided to remain impassive (ie do nothing), the claimant's land would still have been flooded. The court rejected the proposition that, in the instant case, the defenders, by attending the fire, had thereby assumed responsibility and therefore owed a duty of care to the pursuers. Again, it was preferable to follow the decisions south of the border concerning public bodies, including fire services, where the courts have refrained from imposing an affirmative duty on public authorities to prevent members of the public suffering harm.

As far as the ambulance service is concerned, the question which normally falls to be answered is whether it owes a duty of care to the general public in the way it responds to "999" calls. This important question was considered by the Court of Appeal in *Kent v Griffiths* (2001). In that case the claimant suffered an asthma attack. Her doctor immediately summoned an ambulance to convey her to hospital. The ambulance arrived at the claimant's house unreasonably late, by which time she had suffered brain damage. The court held that the ambulance service should be regarded as part of the health service, in relation to which the law already imposed a duty of care in relation to its treatment of patients. The court drew a distinction between the ambulance service responding to an emergency call and the police or fire service responding to requests for assistance. In the last analysis, the defendants did owe a duty of care to the claimant.

*Kent* was followed in the Outer House case of *Aitken v Scottish Ambulance Service* (2011). There, the pursuer was the mother of a young woman who had suffered an epileptic fit. An ambulance was called by the pursuer's son. However, the ambulance arrived late despite the son being reassured after making the original call that that an ambulance was on its way. The woman died as a result of her fit. Lord Mackay was of the opinion that it would be possible for the pursuer to establish at proof that, by the defenders eliciting information about the deceased's medical history from her brother, advising him that an ambulance was on its way, giving advice as to how his sister was to be treated until the ambulance arrived and, finally, dispatching a rapid response unit, the defenders had established a relationship of proximity with the deceased. In reaching this conclusion the Lord Ordinary set store by the fact that the routine which had been followed by the defenders fell to be categorised as operational in nature as opposed to the exercise of a discretionary policy decision.

Finally, in the first-instance case of *OLL Ltd v Secretary of State for the Home Department* (1997) (which was a striking-out action) it was held that the coastguard did not owe a duty of care to those in danger by negligently misguiding either its own personnel or other people outside its own service in response to an emergency call.

### Roads authorities

Roads can be potentially very dangerous. The design and layout as well as the surface of a public road and also the lack of appropriate warning signs may pose a potential danger to road users. Furthermore, un-gritted roads in winter can be particularly hazardous. To what extent, if any, is a roads authority liable, in terms of the law of negligence, to members of the public who suffer harm by virtue of the way in which such an authority exercises its functions in relation to public roads?

The leading case on the subject is *Stovin* v *Wise (Norfolk County Council third party)* (1994). In that case, the claimant was injured when his motorcycle collided with a car which was driven by the defendant, who was turning out of a side road. The defendant's visibility had been limited because a bank on adjacent railway land obstructed her view of the corner in question. As far as the liability of the highway authority was concerned, the House of Lords rejected the proposition that, because the Highway Act conferred a variety of powers on the highway authority to make roads in its area convenient and safe, this automatically resulted in the law imposing a common-law duty of care to the claimant to remove the obstruction which caused the accident. In determining whether such a duty was owed at common law, it was not simply a question of statutory construction. Rather, one had to have regard to the policy of the statute. Furthermore, if a public authority were to be held liable at common law for failing to exercise a statutory power, it would require to be shown that:

(a) it was irrational not to have exercised that power, so there was, in effect, a public law duty to act; and

(b) there were exceptional grounds for holding that the policy of the statute required compensation to be paid to persons who suffered loss because the power was not exercised.

In the instant case, the question of whether anything should be done about the junction was firmly within the discretion of the highway authority. As the highway authority was not under a duty to effect the work in question, condition (a) was not satisfied. As far as (b) was concerned, the majority of the House also expressed doubt *(obiter)* that even if the authority ought, as a matter of public law, to have done the work, there were any grounds upon it could be said that the public law should give rise to compensate persons who had suffered loss because the relevant function was not performed.

The House of Lords was again required to consider the liability of a highway authority in relation to the law of negligence in *Gorringe* v *Calderdale Metropolitan BC* (2004). In that case the claimant was injured in a road traffic accident. Her vehicle was in a collision with a bus which had been hidden behind a sharp crest in the road until just before the claimant's vehicle reached the top. The layout of the road probably caused the appellant to believe, mistakenly, that the bus was on her side of the road. She

brought an action against the highway authority, claiming, *inter alia*, that
the highway authority owed her a duty of care at common law to institute
proper highway safety measures, including the provision of adequate road
signs. In short, the fundamental question which the House had to answer
was whether the highway authority was liable at common law for its
omission. The House held that the Road Traffic Act 1988, which imposed
a broad duty on highway authorities to prepare and carry out a programme
which was designed to promote and improve road safety, did not create a
common-law duty of care, and thus a private right of action. The above
cases were reviewed by the Court of Appeal in *Sandhar v Department of
Transport* (2005). The claimant's husband lost control of his vehicle on an
icy road and was killed. It was claimed that the highway authority owed
the deceased a common-law duty of care in the law of negligence because
the highway authority had assumed responsibility to perform salting
operations. The court held that in order for an assumption of responsibility
to be sufficient to create a duty of care, a particular relationship with
either an individual or individuals was usually required. An assumption of
responsibility could not be based on a general expectation. Reliance on an
assumption of responsibility was also necessary in order for liability to lie.
However, in the instant case there was no evidence that the deceased had
relied on the highway authority. The highway authority did not, therefore,
owe a duty of care to the deceased at common law.

The leading Scottish case on the potential delictual liability of a roads
authority in relation to road-users is now the Inner House case of *MacDonald
v Aberdeenshire Council* (2014). In that case, the pursuer, the driver of a motor
vehicle, raised an action against a local roads authority, following an accident
whereby she had driven through a crossroads into the path of another
vehicle, the upshot of which was the pursuer was injured and both of her
passengers were killed. The pursuer claimed that the accident had occurred
as a result of the defendant's failure to erect sufficient signage to alert drivers
to the presence of the junction and also to maintain road markings, which
had been worn away by traffic passing over them, over a period of time. The
Lord Ordinary dismissed her action as fundamentally irrelevant, on the basis
that the defender did not owe the pursuer a duty of care to maintain signage
and road markings at the junction. The pursuer reclaimed.

The most important issue which was required to be addressed by the
court was, in effect, whether a common law duty of care, in terms of
the law of negligence, could be carved out of the general power which
was conferred on a local roads authority under s 1(1) of the Roads
(Scotland) Act 1984 to, *inter alia*, manage and maintain roads in its
administrative area.

In dismissing the appeal, the Inner House held that the power which was given to a local authority to mark white lines on the relevant roadway did not imply a duty to do so. The court held that whereas there was sufficient proximity between the parties to found a duty of care in terms of the law of negligence, it was not reasonably foreseeable that an accident was likely to occur at the junction, and, also, it would not be fair, just and reasonable to impose a duty of care on the defender roads authority. Furthermore, the pursuer's averments had failed to set out a sufficiently relevant and specific case against the respondent.

For Lady Paton, if a roads authority knew of the existence of a hazard such as a large crater or sink-hole, Scots law would impose upon the roads authority a common law duty of care which would be owed to users of the road who sustained harm because of the hazard. In turn, Lord Drummond-Young was of the view that as far as Scots law was concerned, a roads authority was liable in terms of the law of negligence for its failure to deal with a hazard that exists on the roads under its control. However, such a duty did not arise from its statutory powers. Rather, its common law liability was based on Roman law. See also *Robinson* v *Borders Council* (2016).

### Social work and education authorities

We now consider the extent to which social work and education authorities owe a duty of care to the public in relation to the performance of their duties. In *X* v *Bedfordshire CC* (1995) the House of Lords was required to determine whether a social work authority owed a common-law duty of care to children to prevent them from being sexually abused by third parties. The House refused to do so. One of the reasons for this was that to impose a duty of care in the law of negligence would encourage social work departments to adopt a defensive attitude to their duties. In the same appeal, the House was required to decide whether an educational authority owed a duty of care to pupils with special needs to assess such needs. The House held that where a school accepted a pupil, it assumed responsibility not only for his physical well-being but also for his educational needs. A duty of care was therefore owed by the authority to the pupil.

The House of Lords case of *Barrett* v *Enfield LBC* (2001) (which was a striking-out action) is instructive in the present context. B had been placed in the care of a local authority. B claimed damages for personal injuries which arose out of the negligence of the local authority. The alleged breaches of duty included the failure to arrange for B's adoption, or to provide him with appropriate and properly monitored placements, or to obtain appropriate psychiatric treatment for him. The House held that public policy considerations which meant that it would not be fair, just or reasonable to impose a common-law duty of care on a local authority when deciding whether or not to take the child into care in respect of suspected child abuse, did not have the same force once B had been taken into care. Another reason for the House allowing the case to go for trial was the fact that, once B had been taken into care, one could ascertain whether the standard of care which the law demanded of the defendant had been attained. In other words, the court's being in a position to ascertain the requisite standard of care which the law demanded of the defendant had a reflexive effect on whether the court should impose a duty of care in terms of the law of negligence.

## The factual duty of care

What we have looked at so far is really the notional, or nominal, duty of care in terms of the law of negligence. That is to say, the court assesses a novel situation and determines whether it can, in law, impose a duty of care on the defender. However, once the court has decided that such a duty exists it must then proceed to ascertain, *on the facts of the case,* whether the defender owes the pursuer a duty of care by actually posing a risk of injury to the pursuer. This point can be neatly illustrated by two leading cases. The first is American.

In *Palsgraf* v *Long Island Railroad Co* (1928), a passenger was running to catch one of the defendant's trains. The defendant's servants, trying to assist the passenger to board it, dislodged a package from the passenger's arms, and it fell upon the rails. The package contained fireworks, which exploded with some violence. The explosion overturned some scales many metres away on the platform. The scales fell upon the plaintiff and injured her. The defendant's servants could not have foreseen that their act of negligence could have had such consequences to the plaintiff. Judge Cardozo, speaking for the majority of the court, held that there was no liability because there was no negligence to the plaintiff. In his view, negligence was required to be founded upon the relation between the parties which must depend upon the foreseeability of harm to the person who was actually injured, not someone else.

The Scottish equivalent of *Palsgraf* is the leading case of *Bourhill* v *Young* (1942). There, a pregnant fishwife had just alighted from a tram, when she heard the sound of a road accident. The accident had been caused by the negligence of a motorcyclist, John Young, who was overtaking the tram in which Mrs Bourhill had been travelling. Young negligently collided with a car which was turning right and into his direction of travel. Mrs Bourhill did not see the accident taking place but, nevertheless, she suffered nervous shock. The House of Lords held that, whereas motorists and cyclists who use the roads owe a duty of care to fellow road users and pedestrians, on the facts of the case, the defender did not owe the pursuer a duty of care. The former could not reasonably foresee that someone where Mrs Bourhill was situated when the accident took place, would have sustained nervous shock.

## Conclusions on the duty of care: the general part

What we have been covering thus far can best be described as the "general part" of the duty of care. However, there are certain discrete areas where the courts have had to refine the rules which we have looked at, for a number of reasons, often to reduce the number of claims which can be made. These will now be considered.

### Pure economic loss

The general rule is that there is no liability for causing pure economic loss, that is to say, loss which is not prefaced on physical injury to the pursuer. For example, if I am injured at work by a defective machine as a result of which, I lose the opportunity to do overtime, the loss which I sustain would certainly fall to be described as "economic loss" but not "*pure* economic loss" since the loss derives from physical harm. However, if the local authority archives at which a historian is working are destroyed by a fire which has been negligently started by a clerk who is employed there, the upshot of which is that the historian cannot complete a book which he is in the course of writing and he loses royalty payments from his potential publisher, the loss to the historian would rank as pure economic loss, since none of the historian's property has been damaged. He could not, therefore, recover for his lost royalties.

The rule that the law sets its face against allowing the pursuer to recover for pure economic loss is well illustrated in *Spartan Steel and Alloys Ltd v Martin and Co (Contractors) Ltd* (1972). In this case, the claimants operated a steel factory. The factory obtained electricity by direct cable from a power station. Martin and Co were building contractors. The company used power-driven tools to carry out excavating work. In the course of carrying out such work, a shovel fractured a cable and the electricity supply to the factory was shut off, causing a "melt" to be damaged. It was also established that during the time when the electricity supply was unavailable the claimant could have put more melts through the furnace. The claimants brought an action against Martin in order to recover all damages which had been incurred. However, the Court of Appeal held that the claimants were only entitled to recover for the loss to the particular melt and not for the economic loss or loss of revenue, or productivity, which was represented by a loss of other melts which might have been put through the furnace had the power supply not failed. According to Lord Denning MR (at 38):

> "if claims for pure economic loss were permitted for this particular hazard there would be no end of claims. Some might be genuine but many might be inflated or even false. A machine might not have been in use anyway, but it would be easy to put it down to the cut in supply. It would be well-nigh impossible to check the claims."

Another case which illustrates the same principle is *Murphy v Brentwood District Council* (1990). In that case a local authority carried out its building inspection duties negligently because its building inspectors had failed to notice that a building had been erected on foundations which were of inadequate depth. The upshot of this was that the building's walls began to crack. The claimant sustained financial loss since the house could only be sold at a reduced price. The House of Lords held that since the relevant damage comprised solely injury to the premises themselves, such injury simply ranked as pure economic loss and was, therefore, irrecoverable. In the last analysis, the loss which the claimant had sustained was analogous to the one in which Mrs Donoghue, in the case of *Donoghue v Stevenson* (1932) which we have already discussed, had not unwittingly consumed the ginger beer and become ill but, rather, that she had discovered the ginger beer she was about to consume contained the partial remains of a decomposing snail, and she had then discarded the ginger beer.

A more recent illustration of the reluctance of the courts to allow claims for pure economic loss is *McFarlane v Tayside Health Board* (2000). In that case, the pursuers were negligently advised that a vasectomy had rendered the husband infertile. The couple relied on that advice and ceased to take contraceptive precautions. A child was born to them. The couple sued the health board for the financial loss which they would incur in bringing up the child. The House of Lords rejected their claim since such loss ranked as pure economic loss.

## Negligent statements

In the leading case on liability for negligent statements, *Hedley Byrne v Heller* (1964), Lord Pearce stated: "words are more volatile than deeds. They travel fast and far afield. They are used without being expended". In effect, the potential number of people who could be affected by relying on a negligent statement is limitless. An advert which contains negligent advice (for example, that one should invest in certain companies which are in fact unsound) and which is placed in a popular newspaper, could be read and relied on by hundreds of thousands of people. Such an advert which is placed on the Internet could be read by millions of people who could as a consequence sustain financial loss. It is certainly foreseeable that a very large number of people could suffer financial harm in such circumstances. However, the question of liability for unlimited sums of money to an unlimited class of individuals is something that the courts are unwilling to countenance. Therefore, in effect, the courts have had to restrict the potential number of claimants.

In *Hedley Byrne v Heller,* Easypower, a firm, asked Hedley Byrne to do some work for it. In order to ascertain whether Easypower could afford to pay the claimant, Hedley Byrne asked its bank (National Provincial) to enquire of Easypower's bank (Heller), whether Easypower could afford the services of Hedley Byrne. Heller informed Hedley Byrne that Easypower was financially sound but, at the same time, Heller expressly disclaimed liability for the accuracy of the information it gave. Easypower was not, in fact, financially sound and Hedley Byrne lost money in carrying out work for Easypower. Hedley Byrne therefore sued Heller, and the House of Lords held that in the absence of a disclaimer, the defendant would have been liable. However, the judges differed in their approaches as to when liability would lie. According to Lord Morris (at 502 and 503), a duty of care would arise if someone possessed of special skill undertakes, quite irrespective of a contract, to apply that skill. However, Lord Devlin was of the view that in order for a duty of care to arise, the relationship between the maker of the negligent statement and the recipient, must be equivalent to that existing under a contract. That is to say, the relationship must be close. The House was generally of the view that there must be some assumption of responsibility on the part of the maker of the statement, and also reliance on the part of the recipient. In the previously discussed case of *Caparo v Dickman* (1990) Lord Oliver was of the view that in order to be liable for the making of a negligent statement, the necessary relationship between the defender and the pursuer required to have four features:

(1) the advice is required for a purpose, which is either specific or generally described, which is made known to the adviser at the time the advice is given;

(2) the defender knows that the advice will be communicated to the advisee, either individually or as a member of an ascertained class in order that it should be used by the advisee for that purpose;

(3) the defender knows that the advice is likely to be acted upon without independent enquiry; and

(4) the pursuer acts on the advice.

However, it is not sufficient that the defender knows that his advice will be relied on: *Galoo Ltd* v *Bright Graham Murray* (1994). Generally speaking, there will be no liability for statements which are made on a purely social occasion, since the maker of the statement implicitly accepts no responsibility for the statement: *Chaudhry* v *Prabhakar* (1989). It is also critical that the defender knows that the pursuer will be likely to rely on the statement without obtaining independent advice: *Smith* v *Eric S Bush Ltd* (1989). Moreover, it is not essential that the person, to whom the statement is made, solely relies on the statement and thereby incurs a loss: *JEB Fasteners Ltd* v *Marks Bloom and Co* (1983). Furthermore, it is not necessary that the statement be made directly to the person who sustains the loss in question. That is to say, the statement can be made to a third party who relies on the statement and acts on it, to the detriment of the pursuer: *Spring* v *Guardian Assurance* (1994). This point is further illustrated in the House of Lords case of *White* v *Jones* (1995). In that case, following a family quarrel, the claimants, who were the daughters of a testator, were disinherited by him. However, there was reconciliation between the testator and his daughters. The former, therefore, instructed his solicitors to amend his will in order to allow his daughters to inherit under the will. However, the solicitors negligently delayed in implementing the testator's instructions. The will remained unamended when the testator died, the upshot of which is that the intended beneficiaries failed to inherit under the will. The beneficiaries sued the solicitors in tort. By a majority, the House held that the defendant solicitors owed the claimants a duty of care in terms of the law of negligence.

Lord Goff (with whom the majority of the House agreed) was of the opinion that the *Hedley Byrne* principle of assumption of responsibility by the defendant solicitors to their client should be extended to include an assumption of responsibility to the disappointed beneficiaries.

### Psychiatric injury (nervous shock)

According to Professor Fleming in *The Law of Torts* (9th edn, 1998, p 73) if the law were to treat nervous shock in the same way as external injuries from physical impact, this would open up a wide field of imaginary claims. The law must, therefore, impose arbitrary limitations before it can admit claims for nervous shock.

It is usual for the courts to divide victims of nervous shock into primary victims and secondary victims. As a general rule, the courts will only allow one to recover for psychiatric injury as a reaction to a traumatic event such as an industrial or road accident. The only exception to this is that, in certain circumstances, one can recover in relation to psychiatric injury which is caused by stress at work: see, for example, *Fraser v State Hospitals Board for Scotland* (2001).

It should be stressed that the courts will only allow one to recover either as a primary or secondary victim of nervous shock, if one has sustained a recognised psychiatric injury by virtue of the defender's negligent conduct. In other words, one cannot recover in respect of emotional distress, grief, anger or worry.

### Primary victims

In order that one can recover as a primary victim of nervous shock, one must physically participate, or be actively involved, in the very events which cause the psychiatric injury: *Salter v UB Frozen and Chilled Foods Ltd* (2003). In the case of *Dooley v Cammell Laird Ltd* (1951) the claimant was operating a crane which was being used to unload a ship. The crane rope snapped and the load which was being carried plummeted into the hold of the ship where the plaintiff's colleagues were working. The claimant sustained nervous shock as a result and successfully sued his employers.

The leading case on the subject of primary victims of nervous shock is now *Page v Smith* (1996). In this case the claimant, who was suffering from a condition known as chronic fatigue syndrome, was involved in a minor road accident. He was physically uninjured. His condition became permanent as a result of the accident. He successfully claimed damages in respect of this. The House of Lords refused to draw a distinction between psychiatric injury and physical injury. Essentially, the House of Lords held that notwithstanding the fact that the type of injury which the claimant sustained was not reasonably foreseeable, given the fact that physical injury to the claimant's person was, indeed, foreseeable, the law should not draw a distinction between these forms of injury as far as liability in negligence was concerned. It sufficed simply that some form of physical injury was foreseeable.

## Secondary victims

The vast majority of claims relating to nervous shock concern secondary victims, that is to say, those who have witnessed a traumatic event and have sustained harm as a consequence.

The leading case on this subject is now *Alcock* v *Chief Constable of South Yorkshire* (1991). There, the defendant was responsible for policing a football match at the Hillsborough Stadium. Overcrowding in part of the stadium was caused by the negligence of the police. Ninety-five people were crushed to death. Many more people were seriously injured. Live pictures of the harrowing event were broadcast on television. The claimants were either all related to, or were friends of the spectators who were involved in the disaster. Some people witnessed the traumatic events from other parts of the stadium. Others saw the events on television. However, all claimants alleged that they had suffered nervous shock. The House of Lords held that in order to succeed it was necessary for the claimants to show that the injury sustained was reasonably foreseeable and also that the relationship between the claimant and the defendant was sufficiently proximate. As far as the latter was concerned, the relationship between the claimants and the victims had to be one of both love and affection. Such a degree of affection would be assumed in certain cases, such as between parent and child or husband and wife. In other cases, however, the requisite affection would require to be proved. This would be the case in respect of remoter relationships such as cousins. Furthermore, the House of Lords held that the claimant was required to show propinquity (or closeness) in terms of time and space to the accident or its immediate aftermath.

The Inner House case of *Robertson* v *Forth Road Bridge Joint Board (No 2)* (1994) illustrates the application of the conditions precedent for recovery in respect of psychiatric injury as laid down by the House in *Alcock*. In *Robertson* both the pursuer, Robertson, and a colleague, Rough, were working on the Forth Road Bridge. Rough noticed that a large piece of metal was lying on a carriageway of the bridge. He, therefore, enlisted the aid of another colleague, Smith, to remove the sheet. However, because of the size of the sheet, it could not be accommodated within their transit van. Therefore, it was decided that the sheet should be placed on top of the van and that Smith should sit on top of the sheet in order to prevent it falling off during the period the van was in motion. Rough followed the van in another vehicle. As the van was approaching the end of the bridge, a gust of wind blew Smith and the metal sheet off the bridge. Smith was killed. Both Robertson and Rough sued their employers. The pursuers claimed that they had sustained nervous shock in the workplace. Since it is well-established law that an employer owes a common law duty of care to take reasonable measures to secure the safety of employees in the workplace, the pursuers claimed that the defender owed them a duty of care. However, the Inner House, following *White*, rejected their claim. In order for the pursuers to succeed, it was not sufficient that they had witnessed a traumatic event in the workplace. Indeed, there was no separate category of nervous shock in the workplace. The pursuers were secondary victims of nervous shock, in that they had simply witnessed the accident, in contradistinction to having physically participated in the traumatic events. Therefore, the ordinary rules governing secondary victims applied. Since there was not a close emotional bond between the pursuers and the deceased, Smith, the former failed in their action against the defenders.

The Hillsborough disaster formed the basis of the House of Lords case of *White* v *Chief Constable of South Yorkshire* (1998). In this case, police officers brought an action against their employer. They claimed that they had sustained psychiatric injury in tending to the victims of the tragedy. By a majority, the House rejected their claim. It was held that the police who attended the stadium and had witnessed the traumatic events, ranked simply as secondary victims of nervous shock. As such, the House held that they should be treated no differently to other secondary victims. Furthermore, the fact that the claimants were employed at the time the accident took place was irrelevant.

The application of the law relating to secondary victims of nervous shock following *Alcock* and *White*, is seen in *Keen* v *Tayside Contracts* (2003). In that case the pursuer, a road worker, had been instructed by his supervisor to attend the scene of a road accident. The pursuer witnessed badly crushed and burned bodies. He suffered psychiatric injury as a consequence. He sued his employers, in essence, for having exposed him to such traumatic circumstances. He failed in his action, on the basis that his injury was simply caused by him witnessing the traumatic event. In other words, he ranked in the eye of the law as a secondary victim. He was not related to any of the victims. Therefore, his action failed.

Whereas, normally, the courts are only prepared to allow a pursuer who has actually witnessed traumatic events to recover, in some circumstances a secondary victim of psychiatric injury has succeeded if he has simply witnessed the immediate aftermath of the accident. In the leading case of *McLoughlin* v *O'Brian* (1983) the claimant's husband and children were seriously injured after their car collided with a vehicle which had been driven negligently by the defendant. The claimant suffered psychiatric injury on seeing her family lying injured in hospital, two hours after the accident occurred. The House of Lords held that the claimant could recover damages against the defendant, in that the former had sustained psychiatric injury by witnessing the immediate aftermath of the accident. Furthermore, to allow the claim to succeed would not be contrary to public policy.

However, if the pursuer claims that he has sustained psychiatric injury by witnessing the immediate aftermath of the relevant accident, he requires to prove that he can immediately associate the relevant victim with the accident scene. This point is graphically illustrated in the Inner House case of *Young* v *MacVean* (2015). In that case, the pursuer, who was the mother of a pedestrian who had been killed by a driver who was driving dangerously, saw the immediate aftermath of the accident. However, at that point, she did not suspect that her son had been involved in the accident. She was told shortly afterwards by the police that her son had been killed. She claimed that she could recover against the negligent driver on the grounds that she had witnessed the immediate aftermath of the accident. However, it was held that for the pursuer to succeed it was necessary that she should come upon the scene of the accident in full knowledge of her son's involvement in it. The pursuer, therefore, failed in her action.

### The duty of care and affirmative action

To what extent, if any, does the law impose a duty of care on the defender for simply failing to take appropriate action in respect of someone who is in need of help? The general rule is that the law refrains from imposing an affirmative duty on the defender. However, there are certain situations where the law does impose a duty on the defender to take affirmative action.

The law imposes a duty of care on the defender not to allow his property to become a known source of danger to neighbouring proprietors: *Sedleigh-Denfield* v *O'Callaghan* (1940); *Goldman* v *Hargrave* (1967); and *Leakey* v *National Trust* (1980).

The law will also require a person, who stands in a particular relationship with the pursuer, to protect him from harm: *Watson* v *British Boxing Board of Control* (2001). The relationships of parent–child, employer–employee, occupier of land– visitor and school–pupil have all attracted a duty of care on the person who exercised the relevant control. See also *Rice* v *Secretary of State for Trade and Industry* (2007).

Again, if, through my conduct, I encourage the pursuer to rely on me and then I negligently conduct a rescue, I am liable to the pursuer: *Christchurch Drainage Board* v *Brown* (1987). Sometimes the assumption of responsibility alone on the part of the defender towards the pursuer grounds liability for pure omissions: *White* v *Jones* (1995).

The defender may come under a duty to take affirmative action if he creates a danger: *Mooney* v *Lanark County Council* (1954).

Finally, there is some Commonwealth authority to the effect that if the defender derives some economic advantage from his relationship with the pursuer, the former owes an affirmative duty of care to the latter: *Crocker* v *Sundance Northwest Resorts Ltd* (1988).

## (2) STANDARD OF CARE

Once it has been established that the defender owes a duty of care to the pursuer it is necessary to ascertain whether that duty of care has been breached. Whether the defender has failed to attain the standard of care which the law demands of him is judged objectively: that is to say, no account is taken of individual disabilities or idiosyncrasies, with the exception of children, who are judged in terms of the standard of children of the age of the defender. The leading case on this point is *Nettleship* v *Weston* (1971). In that case a learner driver was held to be required to attain the same standard of driving as an ordinary competent driver.

The courts take into account a number of factors in order to decide whether the defender has been negligent. These are now discussed.

### The state of current knowledge

Where relevant, the courts take into account the state of current knowledge to determine whether the defender has failed to attain the standard of care which the law demands of him. The leading case relating to the state of current knowledge is *Roe* v *Minister of Health* (1954). In that case the claimant went into hospital for a minor operation. He was given a spinal injection. The fluid which was used for the injection was kept in an ampoule (a very small glass container) which, in turn, was kept in a phenol solution. However, at that time it was not known that phenol could seep into an ampoule, through invisible cracks. The claimant was paralysed from the waist downwards. He sued the Minister of Health who was responsible for the hospital concerned. His action failed because the defendant's hospital had not breached its standard of care, since it had acted in a way in which any other reasonable hospital would have acted in the situation.

## The magnitude of risk

The greater the risk of injury from the activity which is the subject-matter of the action, the greater the amount of precautions the defender is required to take. In *Blyth v Birmingham Waterworks Co* (1856) the defendant water board laid a water main which was 18 inches in depth. One year there was an extremely severe frost which penetrated the ground as far as the water main. The main burst and flooded the plaintiff's premises. It was held that the water board was not negligent because it had taken reasonable precautions in the circumstances. That the law only requires the defender to take reasonable precautions in the circumstances is neatly illustrated in the House of Lords case of *Glasgow Corporation v Muir* (1943). In that case, a church party obtained permission from the manageress of the defender's tearoom, to consume packed meals which members of the party had brought with them. As a tea urn was being carried by adult members of the group to the tearoom, one of the adults lost his grip on one of the handles of the urn, the upshot of which was that six children were scalded. The action against the defender was founded on the alleged negligence of the manageress who had given permission to the party to use the tearoom. However, the House held that since the manageress had no reason to anticipate that such an accident would take place on her granting permission to the party to use the tearoom, there was no duty which was incumbent on her to take precautions to prevent the occurrence of the accident. In the last analysis, the defender had not been negligent.

Another case which illustrates the same point is *Bolton v Stone* (1951). In that case the plaintiff, while standing on a quiet suburban highway outside her home, was struck by a cricket ball. The plaintiff was situated 100 yards from the batsman and the ball had cleared a 17-foot fence which was situated 78 yards from him. Similar hits had occurred only about six times in the previous 30 years. The House of Lords held that since the likelihood of injury was small, the plaintiff had not established that the defendant had breached his duty of care towards the claimant. See also *Haley v London Electricity Board* (1964).

## The risk of serious harm

In determining whether the standard of care which the law demands of the defender has not been attained, one takes into account not simply the likelihood that the accident will occur but, rather, the seriousness of the injury, should an accident occur. The leading case is *Paris v Stepney Borough Council* (1950). There, a one-eyed worker was injured while at work. He claimed that his employers should have provided, and also required him to use goggles while he was working. It was proved that there was no greater likelihood that an accident would befall the claimant than a worker with normal sight. However, the House of Lords held that since the consequences of an injury to the claimant were graver, extra precautions were necessary.

## The utility of the defender's activity

The social utility, or usefulness, of the relevant activity which is the subject-matter of the action, is taken into account. The greater the utility, the less likely it is that the court will hold that the relevant standard of care has been breached. The leading case is *Watt* v *Hertfordshire County Council* (1954). The claimant was a fireman. One day his station received a call that a woman was trapped under a heavy lorry as a result of a road accident. A jack was required to lift the vehicle. Two of the claimant's colleagues threw a heavy jack on to a lorry in which they were to travel. However, the lorry was not designed to carry a jack. During the journey the jack rolled away from its original position and injured the claimant. It was held that the defendants had not been negligent. In reaching its decision, the court took into account the social utility of the journey, namely the rescuing of an injured person. However, simply because the defender is involved in an activity which has some social worth does not automatically exonerate him from the need to take care. This point was decided in *Ward* v *London County Council* (1938). There, the driver of a fire engine was held to have been negligent in driving though a red traffic light and injuring the claimant. It was held that the defendant could not use the reason that he was involved in a journey of social worth as an excuse for his breach of duty of care.

## The practicality of precautions

The easier it is to take measures to counteract the risk, the more likely it is that the courts will hold that the appropriate duty of care has been breached. In *Latimer* v *AEC Ltd* (1953) the floor of the defendant's factory was flooded by an exceptionally heavy rainstorm. Oil which was kept in troughs was washed out on to the factory floor. The defendant put sawdust on the floor but there was not enough sawdust to cover the entire factory floor. The claimant, who was working on the floor, slipped and injured himself. He sued the defendant. It was held that the defendant was not liable since he had taken all appropriate precautions, short of closing the factory. However, this decision has been criticised on the ground that commercial profitability was given too much prominence by the court over the personal security of the workers. It may well be that on similar facts, a court would reach a different decision today.

## Emergency situations

If the defender is placed in a sudden emergency situation which is not of his own creation, his actions must be judged in the light of those circumstances. In *Ng Chun Pui* v *Lee Chuen Tat* (1988) it was held that the driver of a coach who had braked, swerved and skidded when another vehicle, had cut across his path had acted in an emergency.

## Children

As far as children are concerned, one takes into account what degree of care a child of the particular age of the defender can be expected to take: *Yachuk* v *Oliver Blais Co Ltd* (1949). See also *Mullins* v *Richards* (1998).

## (3) CAUSATION

Finally, in order to succeed in a negligence claim it is necessary to prove that the negligent act in question actually caused the relevant injury or damage which is the subject-matter of the action. There are two main tests which the courts use in order to ascertain whether the defender's conduct caused the loss in question, namely:

(a) the "but for" test; and

(b) the "material contribution" test.

## (a) The "but for" test

The question which the court asks itself here is: but for the negligent act of the defender, would the pursuer have been harmed? The leading case on the subject is *Barnett* v *Chelsea and Kensington Hospital Management Committee* (1969). In that case, Barnett, a night watchman, called early one morning at the defendant's hospital. He had been complaining of sickness. Unbeknown to Barnett, he had been deliberately poisoned.

However, the doctor in charge refused to see him and suggested that he should consult his GP in the morning. Unfortunately, Barnett died before he could visit his GP. Barnett's widow sued the hospital in negligence. However, she failed in her action, since it was proved that her husband would have died, in spite of any medical assistance which he could have been given at the time when he presented himself at hospital. In other words, the defendant had not caused Barnett's death.

### (b) The "material contribution" test

As far as this test is concerned, the courts are willing to accept that the defender has caused the relevant damage if his negligent act materially contributes to, as opposed to being the sole cause of, the accident. The test is well illustrated in *Wardlaw* v *Bonnington Castings* (1956). In that case, the pursuer's illness was caused by an accumulation of dust in his lungs. The dust in question came from two sources. The defenders (Wardlaw's employers) were not responsible for one of the sources, but they could have prevented (and were therefore negligent concerning) the other. However, the dust from the latter source (in other words, the "illegal" dust) was not, in itself, sufficient to cause the disease. The pursuer succeeded in his action because the "illegal" dust had made a material contribution to his injury: see also *McGhee* v *NCB* (1972).

It is also important to emphasise that the pursuer requires to prove on a balance of probabilities that the negligent act of the defender caused his injury: *Wilsher* v *Essex Area Health Authority* (1988).

### Departure from the "rules"

In *Fairchild* v *Glenhaven Funeral Services* (2002) it was held that in certain circumstances one could depart from the well-established rules governing factual causation. In that case, Fairchild had been employed at different times, and for different periods, by more than one employer: E1 and E2. Both E1 and E2 had been subject to a duty to take reasonable care to prevent F from inhaling asbestos dust. Both E1 and E2 failed to do so and, as a consequence, F contracted mesothelioma. On the current limits of scientific knowledge, Fairchild was unable to prove, on the balance of probabilities, that his condition was the result of inhaling asbestos dust during his employment by one, or other or both, of E1 or E2. However, the House of Lords held that, in certain special circumstances, the court could depart from the established test of legal causation and treat a lesser degree of causal connection as sufficient, namely that the defendant's breach of duty had materially contributed to causing the disease by materially increasing the risk that the disease would be contracted. Any injustice that might be involved in imposing liability in such circumstances was heavily outweighed by the injustice of denying redress to the victim.

The law was taken further in the House of Lords case of *Barker* v *Corus (UK) Ltd* (2006) in which it was held that, on facts similar to those which formed the basis of *Fairchild,* it was appropriate to apportion liability between defendants in accordance with the degree of risk to which the defendants exposed the claimant by virtue of their negligence. As far as liability in respect of mesothelioma is concerned, s 3 of the Compensation Act 2006 reverses *Barker* and makes the person who is at fault, jointly and severally liable (ie *in solidum*) with any other person.

In both *Fairchild* and *Barker,* the employee was exposed to contamination from an "illegal" source or sources, in the workplace. Indeed, the key requirement in *Fairchild* was that *all* the exposures were related to employment, and were due to breaches of duty, and also that it was impossible to prove which exposure had caused the disease. However, in *Sienkiewicz* v *Greif (UK) Ltd* (2011) the question which fell to be answered by the House of Lords was whether the learning in *Fairchild* and *Barker* was applicable to a situation where only *one* source to which the claimant had been exposed was work related, and the other source was not. In *Sienkiewicz,* the claimant's mother had been exposed to asbestos dust between 1966 and 1984 during the period of her employment with the defendant. However, due to the location of her home, she had also been exposed to low levels of asbestos in the general environment. The House held that the learning in *Fairchild* and *Barker* applied to the facts of the case and, therefore, the defendant was liable.

The application of the "material contribution" test was discussed in the recent Privy Council case of *Williams* v *Bermuda Hospitals Board* (2016). In that case, the claimant, W, had gone into B's hospital suffering from acute appendicitis. W had an appendectomy later in the same day. However, there were complications involving injury to his heart and lungs as a result of sepsis which had developed incrementally over approximately six hours. The trial judge held that there had been a culpable delay of at least two hours. However, W had failed to prove that the delay had caused the complications. The Court of Appeal reversed the judge's decision on causation. W successfully appealed against that decision. The Privy Council rejected B's contention that the learning in *Bonnington Castings* and *McGhee* was inapplicable in a situation (as was the case in the present appeal) where the factors which could have caused the relevant harm operated successively, as opposed to cumulatively. The Privy Council in deciding in favour of W made brief reference to the "doubling the risk" test which had sometimes been used, or advocated, as a tool in deciding questions of causation. However, the Privy Council cautioned against use of this test.

However, it is difficult, in some cases, to predict at the outset whether the court will employ the "but for" test or the material contribution test, in order to determine whether the unlawful conduct of the defender caused harm to the pursuer. This is illustrated in the recent case of *Chetwynd* v *Tunmore* (2016). In that case the claimants alleged that the defendants had excavated lakes on their land which had adversely affected the land which was owned by the claimants, and, in particular, the water levels in fishing lakes which were situated on the claimants' land. *Inter alia*, the claimants based their claim on nuisance and in negligence. The defendants claimed that it was for the claimants to prove, on the balance of probabilities, that the defendants' abstraction of water by the excavation of the lakes on their land was the effective cause of the alleged loss or damage which resulted from the reduced water level in the claimants' lakes. The defendants went on to argue that it was for the claimants to prove that other potential causes did not cause the crucial reduction in the water levels. In short, the defendants argued that, in determining whether the alleged unlawful conduct of the defendants had caused the water reduction in the claimants' lakes, the court should employ the "but for" test. However, the claimants argued that it was sufficient to establish causation if they proved that the excavation of the lakes on the defendants' land had materially contributed to the reduction of water levels. Reddihough J observed that a common feature of the cases (his Lordship cited *Bonnington Castings* and *McGhee*) where the "material contribution" test had been applied in preference to the "but for" test, was that there was one agent, or condition, which had been brought about by cumulative or consecutive causes, one of which involved fault on the part of the defendant, which resulted in the relevant disease or injury. As far as the instant case was concerned, the claimants argued that a similar approach should be adopted. In short, they argued that even if there were other causes of the reduction in water levels, in their lakes, they would succeed in their action against the defendants if the claimants could prove, on a balance of probabilities, that the excavation of the lakes on the defendants' land had made a material contribution (ie more than *de minimis*) to the reduction of water levels on the claimants' land. However, in the opinion of his Lordship, the approach of the courts in the disease and clinical negligence cases could not be applied in the instant case where the relevant facts were quite different. In the last analysis, Reddihough J decided that the "but for" test fell to be applied in preference to the "material contribution" test, that is to say, that the claimants were required to prove that it was more likely than not that, but for the excavation of the lakes on the defendants' land, any consequent loss or damage would not have occurred. Since the claimants failed to prove causation on the application of the former test, they failed in their action.

## Legal causation (remoteness of damage)

The law will not allow the pursuer to recover in relation to injury which is deemed to be too remote. Consider the following scenario. Allan, a builder, negligently builds the foundations of Tom's house: the foundations are too shallow. Soon, cracks develop in the walls and the building becomes dangerous. Tom has to leave the house and move into rented accommodation in a poorer part of the town. While Tom is living there he is mugged by a gang and is injured. Could Tom sue Allan in respect of his personal injuries? The answer to that question would be that the law would probably regard his injuries as too remote. How do the courts ascertain whether the damage in question is too remote? There are two competing rules, namely:

(1) the "directness" test; and

(2) the "foreseeability" test.

### (1) The "directness" test

The leading case on the directness test is *Re Polemis* (1921). In that case, a chartered vessel was unloading in Casablanca. The servants of the charterers negligently let a plank of wood drop into the hold of the ship. Part of the cargo was a quantity of petrol which had leaked out of its containers. The fall of the plank caused a spark, which in turn caused the petrol to explode. The ship was completely destroyed. The charterers were held liable by the Court of Appeal for the loss because such loss was the direct consequence of the act of negligence in question.

### (2) The "foreseeability" test

The competing test to the "directness" test is the rule in *The Wagon Mound* (1961). In that case, OT Ltd were charterers of a ship known as the *Wagon Mound* which was moored in a wharf in Sydney, Australia. OT's servants allowed a large quantity of oil to be spilled and it spread to another wharf where another ship was under repair. Sparks from the welding operations in this other part of the harbour fell on to the water.

The oil caught fire and the wharf was damaged. The Privy Council held that while the damage was the direct cause of the spillage in question, it was unforeseeable and so the defendants were not liable. The foresight of the hypothetical reasonable man in the position of the defendant at the time of the accident determined liability. It is the rule in *The Wagon Mound* (1961) which is now favoured by the courts in preference to the rule in *Re Polemis* (1921) as far as the test to determine remoteness of damage in negligence actions is concerned.

### The "thin skull" rule

If I am walking along a pavement one day and I am gently knocked to the ground by a skateboarder and fracture my skull as a consequence because my skull is thinner and therefore more breakable than normal, the skateboarder could not argue by way of defence that my serious injury was not reasonably foreseeable. In other words, in terms of remoteness of injury which is sustained by the pursuer, the defender takes the pursuer as he finds him. This is known as the "thin skull" rule. The type of injury, namely a wound to the head, is certainly foreseeable. However, the extent and gravity of the injury is not. Under the rule I can recover the full extent of my injuries which directly derive from a state of affairs which was reasonably foreseeable.

A good illustration of the application of the "thin skull" rule is seen in *Smith v Leech Brain and Co* (1962). In that case, the plaintiff suffered a burn on his lip as a result of the defendant's negligence. The burn caused the claimant to contract cancer because the tissues of his lips were in a premalignant state. He died within 3 years. The defendants argued that they were not responsible for his death, as it could not have been foreseen. It was held, however, that the principle that the defendant had to "take his victim as he found him" applied. The defendants were therefore held liable.

### Breaking the chain of causation

It sometimes happens that an intervening act occurs between the negligent act of the defender and the harm which the pursuer sustains. The effect of such an intervening act may, in the eye of the law, eclipse the defender's negligent act, in which case the defender would not be liable for the relevant harm. If the intervening act does break the chain of causation between the negligent act of the defender and the harm which the pursuer sustains, such an intervening act would be said to be a *novus actus interveniens*. On the other hand, the intervening act may be deemed to have a causal link with the defender's negligent (that is, a *causa causans*) conduct, the upshot of which is that the defender would be liable for any harm accruing from that intervening act. How do the courts decide whether an intervening act falls to be categorised as a *novus actus interveniens* or, on the other hand, a *causa causans*? The short answer is that the courts have never felt comfortable in determining this problem. The courts have approached it on a case-by-case basis.

Sometimes, if the intervening act is the natural and reasonable consequence of the original act of negligence it breaks the chain of causation: *The Oropesa* (1943); *Rouse* v *Squires* (1973). At other times, if the intervening conduct is deemed to be unreasonable, it breaks the chain of causation. For example, in *McKew* v *Holland and Hannen and Cubitts (Scotland) Ltd* (1970) the pursuer sustained an injury in an accident which was caused by the defender's negligence. The pursuer's leg would become numb and tend to give way without warning. One day, when he was descending stairs, he felt his leg give way. The pursuer jumped to the bottom of the stairs and he sustained further injury. The House of Lords held that the pursuer had acted unreasonably in placing himself in such a position that he could do little to save himself if his leg gave way. Furthermore, such unreasonable conduct constituted a *novus actus interveniens* and, therefore, broke the chain of causation between the defendant's negligent act and the injury sustained by jumping down the stairs.

Finally, in some cases, foreseeability is the touchstone which is employed by the courts to ascertain whether the chain of causation has been broken. For example, in *Donaghy* v *NCB* (1957) a young miner sued his employers in respect of injuries he received when a detonator, which had been left in the pursuer's workplace in breach of relevant legislation, exploded when he hit it with a hammer. The Inner House of the Court of Session held that the act of the pursuer constituted a *novus actus interveniens* since the pursuer's act was not reasonably foreseeable.

## Essential Facts

- In order to ascertain whether the defender is liable in law for damage which he has negligently caused, the court must decide whether the defender owes the pursuer a duty of care.
- Currently, the courts employ an incremental test to ascertain whether a duty of care exists.

- The court must decide whether, on the facts of the particular case, a duty of care was owed.
- The general rule is that there is no liability for pure economic loss.
- In order that one can recover for harm which is caused by a negligent statement there must be assumption of responsibility on the part of the maker of the statement and reliance on that statement.
- The courts divide victims of nervous shock into primary and secondary victims.
- A primary victim is directly involved in the relevant traumatic event.
- A secondary victim merely witnesses the event.
- In order to recover if one is a secondary victim, one must witness the events with one's own unaided senses and have a bond of love and affection with the person injured.
- Generally, the courts do not impose a duty of care for one failing to act.
- Whether the defender has failed to attain the standard of care which the law demands of him is judged objectively.
- In order to recover in negligence it must be proved that the negligent act in question caused the damage and that the injury is not too remote.

## Essential Cases

**Donoghue v Stevenson (1932)**: established the "foreseeeability" test in relation to the duty of care in the law of negligence.

**Caparo v Dickman (1990)**: established the "incremental" test in relation to the duty of care.

**Bourhill v Young (1942)**: illustrates the principle that it must be proved that the defender owes the pursuer a factual duty of care.

**Spartan Steel and Alloys Ltd v Martin and Co (Contractors) Ltd (1972)**: no liability for pure economic loss.

**Hedley Byrne v Heller (1964)**: liability lies for making of negligent statement if the maker assumes responsibility for its accuracy and the recipient relies on the statement.

**Page v Smith (1996)**: no distinction in principle between physical and psychiatric injury as far as primary victims of nervous shock are concerned.

**Alcock v Chief Constable of South Yorkshire (1991)**: in order to recover as a secondary victim of nervous shock, one must establish a bond of love and affection with the victim and perceive the traumatic event with one's own unaided senses.

**Nettleship v Weston (1971)**: whether the defender has failed to attain the standard of care which the law demands of him is judged objectively.

**Barnett v Chelsea and Kensington Hospital Management Committee (1969)**: the pursuer must prove a causal link between the defender's negligent act and the former's injury.

**Wardlaw v Bonnington Castings (1956)**: the pursuer can succeed if he can prove the defender's negligence.

**Wilsher v Essex Area Health Authority (1988)**: the pursuer requires to prove that the negligent act of the defender caused the former's injury on a balance of probabilities.

**Fairchild v Glenhaven Funeral Services (2002)**: in certain circumstances one can depart from the well-established rules governing factual causation.

**Barker v Corus (UK) Ltd (2006)**: on facts similar to those which formed the basis of *Fairchild* it is appropriate to apportion liability between defendants in accordance with the degree of risk to which the defendants exposed the claimant to by virtue of their negligence.

# 3 THE LAW OF NUISANCE

The law recognises that the occupier of land (for example, by virtue of being the owner, tenant or subtenant of the land) has the right to enjoy the occupation of that land. However, my neighbour has similar rights in relation to the land he occupies. The manner in which my neighbour chooses to use his land may conflict with the way in which I wish to use mine. For example, my neighbour may wish to play his piano all hours of the day. However, I may choose to sit at home in the evening and read, the upshot of which is that I am annoyed by the noise coming from my neighbour's house. We can see here that my neighbour's right to use his property in the manner in which he chooses conflicts with my own. What the law does is to attempt to strike a reasonable balance between these conflicting rights. This conflict is pragmatically resolved by the courts imposing a duty on an occupier of land not to use his land in such an unreasonable way that the enjoyment of another is prejudiced. This duty is sometimes expressed in the Latin maxim *sic utere tuo ut alienum non laedas* (so use your property that you do not harm your neighbour). The law was neatly summarised by Lord President Cooper in *Watt* v *Jamieson* (1954) when he stated:

> "The balance in all such cases has to be held between the freedom of a proprietor to use his property as he pleases and the duty on a proprietor not to inflict material loss or inconvenience on adjoining proprietors and in every case the answer depends on considerations of fact and degree."

*Watt* emphasises that whether any given state of affairs constitutes an actionable nuisance is a question of fact and degree. For example, the louder the noise or the more intense the smoke which emanate from my neighbour's property, the more likely the courts will categorise the state of affairs as a nuisance in law.

## FACTORS THE COURT TAKES INTO ACCOUNT

We now look at the various factors which require to be taken into account when deciding whether a given state of affairs constitutes a nuisance in law. One should remember at the outset that it is only unreasonable conduct which can be categorised as a nuisance in law (*Baxter* v *Camden London Borough Council* (1999)). In order to ascertain whether any given conduct is unreasonable the law has traditionally focused on the relevant conduct from the viewpoint of the pursuer (*Watt* v *Jamieson* (1954)). Before we go on to itemise what factors a court takes into account, it must be stressed that the factors which are listed are not mechanically applied in every nuisance case. Rather, the courts have tended to emphasise several factors, often to the exclusion of others. Finally, it should also be remembered that the factors which are listed below are not exhaustive. It is open to the courts to introduce other factors.

## Social utility

The social utility or usefulness which is associated with the activity causing the nuisance in question is taken into account by the courts. The gist of this factor is that the more socially useful an activity is, the less likely it is that the court could be willing to castigate the state of affairs complained of as a nuisance (*Harrison* v *Southwark and Vauxhall Water Co* (1891)). Social utility has most commonly featured in the context of industrial nuisances, where the courts have explicitly recognised the social benefits which accrue from factories (see, for example, *Bellew* v *Cement Ltd* (1948)).

However, as far as other forms of activity are concerned, the courts have been less willing to take into account the social utility which accrues from the relevant activity, when determining whether a nuisance exists (see, for example, *Watson* v *Croft Promo Sports Ltd* (2009)). A somewhat revolutionary approach to the application of the concept of social utility in terms of the law of nuisance, was taken by Buckley J in *Dennis* v *MoD* (2003). In that case, the claimants owned and lived on a large estate which was situated in close proximity to RAF Wittering, which is home to the Harrier jet. The Harrier jet is a noisy aircraft; indeed, there is no louder jet. The witnesses who gave evidence to the court described the noise from the aircraft as sometimes "intolerable". The claimants brought an action against the MoD. Buckley J had no hesitation in deciding that the noise in question constituted a nuisance in law. However, it was also beyond dispute that the flying of military aircraft in the manner which was the subject of the action, redounded to the benefit of the public. In short, Britain needs its air force, including aircraft which inevitably cause a great deal of flight noise. However, to weigh this factor in the judicial scales when determining whether a nuisance exists would, in his Lordship's view, have deprived the claimants a remedy under common law. Buckley J went on to state that the growing *corpus* of human rights law dictated that the appropriate remedy, in terms of the law of nuisance, should be that of damages, as opposed to an injunction or a declaration.

However, in the Outer House case of *King* v *Advocate General for Scotland* (2009) Lord Pentland refrained from expressing a view as to whether *Dennis* represented the law of Scotland.

## Motive of the defender

If the relevant state of affairs is generated by the defender simply to punish the pursuer, that is to say it is motivated by spite, the courts are readily inclined to hold that the state of affairs ranks as a nuisance. For example, in the leading case of *Christie* v *Davey* (1893) the claimant's family were musically inclined and frequently practised their instruments to the annoyance of the defendant who retaliated by banging trays on the party wall which separated his house from that of the claimant. It was held that the noise which was generated by the defendant amounted to a nuisance in law, because it was motivated by spite. Similarly, in *Hollywood Silver Fox Farm Ltd* v *Emmett* (1936) the claimant bred foxes on his land. The defendant objected to this practice and caused guns to be fired on the boundary which separated his premises from those of the claimant. It was held that the noise constituted a nuisance in law.

## Locality

The nature of the locality has a bearing on whether a state of affairs can rank as a nuisance in law (*Trotter* v *Farnie* (1830)). The reasoning behind this approach is that if a state of affairs is typical of a given locality, the pursuer would be presumed to have become habituated, at least to some extent, to the nuisance in question. The leading case on the application of the locality factor is *Bamford* v *Turnley* (1862) where Pollock CB stated at 286: "That may be a nuisance in Grosvenor Square, which would be none in Smithfield Market." The Scottish equivalent of *Bramford* is *Inglis* v *Shotts Iron Co* (1881) where the Lord Justice-Clerk stated at 1021: "Things which are forbidden in a crowded urban community may be permitted in the country. What is prohibited in enclosed land may be tolerated in the open."

However, while the courts are less inclined to castigate as a nuisance a state of affairs which is typical of an area, they are not prepared to accord the defender *carte blanche* to create a nuisance. This point was illustrated in *Rushmer* v *Polsue and Alfieri Ltd* (1906), where the House of Lords upheld the grant of an injunction in relation to noise from premises, notwithstanding the fact that it was habitual practice for certain premises, in the relevant area to operate their presses during the night.

It is important to note that if the adverse state of affairs injures the pursuer's property, the locality principle is redundant. In *St Helens Smelting Co* v *Tipping* (1865) vapours from the defendant's works damaged the claimant's property. It was held irrelevant that the claimant's property was situated in an industrial area.

A somewhat controversial area relating to locality and the law of nuisance is the extent, if any, to which planning permission should be taken into account by the court when it is attempting to assess the nature of the relevant locality. The leading case is the Supreme Court case of *Coventry* v *Lawrence* (2014). The facts of the case were simple. Planning permission was granted in 1979 to construct a sports complex and stadium. At first, speedway racing took place. Later, banger and stock-car racing were introduced. Planning permission was subsequently granted for other motor-related sports. The claimants, who lived in close proximity to the stadium, became affected by the noise from the stadium. They raised an action against the organisers of the motor sports, amongst others. At first instance, it was held that the noise which emanated from the stadium constituted a nuisance in law. On appeal, the Court of Appeal held that both the grant of planning permission, coupled with the implementation of that permission, had the effect of changing the character of the land for the purposes of the law of nuisance, the upshot of which was the noise in question did not rank as a nuisance. The claimants successfully appealed to the Supreme Court. Unfortunately, the decision of the court lacked clarity as to the effect of planning permission in terms of determining the nature of a locality in a nuisance action. The court held that planning permission was not a major determinant of liability in a nuisance action. However, the grant of planning permission could be of some relevance in a nuisance action. The court did not, however, directly address or answer the question as to whether the grant of planning permission could change the character of the land for the purposes of the law of nuisance.

However, there has been no Scottish case where the court has had to address the inter-relationship between planning policy at either national or local level or planning permission and the law of nuisance. In the view of the author, it has no relevance.

## Duration and intensity

What this means is the longer an adverse state of affairs lasts, and also the more intense its nature, the more likely that it will be categorised a nuisance. In the leading case of *Bamford* v *Turnley* (1862) Pollock CB stated at 292:

"A clock striking the hour, or a bell ringing for some domestic purpose, may be a nuisance if unreasonably loud or discordant, of which the jury must alone judge; but although not unreasonably loud, if the owner from some whim or caprice made the clock strike every 10 minutes, or the bell ring continually, I think that a jury would be justified in considering it to be a very great nuisance."

## Time of day

The courts are more inclined to regard night noise a nuisance than noise which takes place during the day (*Bamford* v *Turnley* (1862)). The time of day at which an adverse state of affairs exists is only applicable in relation to noise nuisances and perhaps light nuisance.

## Sensitivity of the pursuer

The courts are unwilling to conclude that a nuisance exists if the pursuer is annoyed by the adverse state of affairs simply because he is oversensitive. In *Heath* v *Brighton Corporation* (1908), a priest complained about the noise and vibrations which emanated from the defendant's premises. The claimant was denied a remedy under the law of nuisance since the sole reason why he was discomfited was because he possessed hypersensitive hearing.

The rule that the courts will not provide relief by way of the law of nuisance to the oversensitive also applies in relation to physical injury to property. For example, in *Robertson* v *Kilvert* (1889) the claimant kept delicate paper in his premises. The paper was damaged by the heat which was generated from the defendant's premises. The claimant failed in his action. More recently, in *Bridlington Relay Ltd* v *Yorkshire Electricity Board* (1965) the claimant company carried on a business of providing a relay system of sound and television broadcasts and erected a mast on its own land for that purpose. The defendant local electricity board began to erect an overhead power line near the mast which would have interfered with the reception of signals. It was held that since the business of the claimant required an exceptional degree of immunity from interference, the action in nuisance failed. Similarly, in *Hunter* v *Canary Wharf Ltd* (1997), the House of Lords held that the interference with the reception of television signals by the presence of a large building did not constitute an actionable nuisance in law.

The above cases were reviewed by the Court of Appeal in *Network Rail Infrastructure Ltd (formerly Railtrack)* v *C J Morris* (2004). In that case, it was claimed that Railtrack's signalling system had caused electromagnetic interference to the electric guitars which were played in the claimant's recording studios situated some 80 metres away. However, the court held that amplified guitars fell to be regarded as extraordinarily sensitive equipment which did not attract the protection of the law of nuisance.

## NEED FOR AN EMANATION FROM DEFENDER'S LAND

In the vast majority of nuisance cases the relevant adverse state of affairs which is the subject-matter of the action will consist of odours, smoke and noise etc which are created on the defender's premises and, in turn, affect the pursuer. The question which we ask here, however, is whether it is, indeed, essential for liability to lie in the law of nuisance, that there is some type of emanation from the defender's premises. There is English authority to the effect that proceedings which are confined to the defendant's premises and pose a real threat to the safety or comfort of the pursuer can rank as a nuisance in law. In *Thomson-Schwab* v *Costaki* (1956) it was held that the sight of prostitutes and their clients entering and leaving the defendant's premises could rank as a nuisance. Similarly, in *Laws* v *Florinplace* (1981) the defendants established a sex shop and cinema in the vicinity of the plaintiff's premises. The plaintiff claimed that the defendant's activities would attract undesirable customers who would threaten family life in the street, in particular that of young girls who might be met with indecent suggestions. Vinelott J was of the view that as far as liability in terms of the private law of nuisance was concerned, there was no need for a physical emanation from the defendant's premises.

The issue of whether one needs some form of physical emanation from the defender's premises was considered again in *Hunter* v *Canary Wharf Ltd* (1997) where, as mentioned above, the appellants claimed damages for interference with the reception of television signals at their home by a very tall tower. The House of Lords held that an action in nuisance failed, on the basis that the mere presence of a building which interfered with the reception of television signals could not rank as a nuisance in law. Unfortunately, there was little discussion as to whether, as far as the law of nuisance in general was concerned, an adverse state of affairs has to comprise a physical emanation from land. However, Lord Goff (at 432) was of the view that, occasionally, activities on the defendant's land are in themselves so offensive to neighbours as to constitute an actionable nuisance.

By way of conclusion, as far as Scots law is concerned, in the absence of modern case law it is suggested that – with the possible exceptions of brothels, sex shops and the like – there requires to be some form of emanation from the defender's premises before a successful action can be brought under the law of nuisance.

## Did the pursuer live in fear of the adverse state of affairs manifesting itself?

In *Blackburn* v *ARC Ltd* (1998) it was held that the fact that the adverse state of affairs may manifest itself at any time, and without warning is a relevant consideration in determining whether a nuisance exists.

## NEED TO PROVE *CULPA*

In order to succeed in a nuisance action, the pursuer requires to prove *culpa*, or fault, on the part of the defender (*RHM* v *Strathclyde Regional Council* (1985)). In the *RHM* case, bakery premises which belonged to the pursuer, were flooded as a result of the collapse of a sewer which was under the control of the local authority defender. Food and packing materials which were stored in the bakery were damaged. The bakery raised an action against the local authority in terms of, among other things, the law of nuisance. The House of Lords held that in order to succeed in an action which was based on nuisance it was necessary for the pursuer to prove *culpa* or fault on the part of the defender. Unfortunately, the House did not discuss the concept in much detail.

However, the Inner House had an opportunity to discuss the concept of *culpa* in *Kennedy* v *Glenbelle* (1996). The pursuers were the heritable proprietors and tenants and occupiers of basement premises. The first defenders engaged the second defenders, a firm of consulting engineers, to advise on, design, direct and also supervise a scheme for the removal of a section or sections of wall within their premises. The pursuers raised an action against the defenders, claiming that as a result of the work which was carried out in the basement, the pursuer's property had subsided. The pursuers claimed that the carrying out of the renovation works in such a way that the pursuer's premises were damaged, amounted to nuisance in law, as well as actionable negligence. As far as nuisance was concerned, the Inner House essentially held that *culpa* could be proved if the defender was shown to be negligent in the common law sense. Second, *culpa* could be established if the defender had acted maliciously. Third, liability would lie if the requisite state of affairs which harms the pursuer is brought about by either the deliberate or reckless act of the defender. Fourth, liability will lie if, through some fault of his, the defender brings into existence a state of affairs which ranks as hazardous. See also *Esso Petroleum Co Ltd* v *Scottish Ministers* (2015).

# WHO MAY BE SUED FOR CREATING A NUISANCE?

(1) The person who creates the nuisance is liable in law (*Watt* v *Jamieson* (1954)). He need have no interest in the land from which the nuisance arises (*Slater* v *McLellan* (1924)).

(2) The occupier of the land from which the nuisance emanates is normally liable in law (*Sedleigh-Denfield* v *O'Callaghan* (1940)). However, the occupier is not liable for an adverse state of affairs which has been created by someone else (for example, a trespasser or by the act of nature) unless the occupier takes insufficient steps to abate the nuisance after he becomes aware, either actually or constructively, of the presence of the nuisance, in which case he will be presumed to have adopted the nuisance. In *Sedleigh-Denfield* a local authority trespassed on the defendant's land and constructed a culvert on a ditch. One of the employees of the defendants knew of the existence of the culvert. Furthermore, the defendants used the culvert to get rid of water from their own property. However, the culvert was not properly constructed and it became blocked with detritus. A heavy thunderstorm caused the ditch to flood. The plaintiff's land was flooded as a consequence. The House of Lords held the defendants liable in nuisance, by virtue of having both continued, and also adopting the nuisance in question. In their Lordships' view, the defendants had continued the nuisance by virtue of failing to take appropriate remedial action after they had become aware (through their servant) of the existence of the nuisance. The nuisance had also been adopted by the defendants using the culvert for their own purposes.

The next important case on the subject of liability in respect of nuisances which are created by others is the interesting Privy Council case of *Goldman* v *Hargrave* (1967). Here, a tall gum tree which was 100 feet high and which was situated on the defendant's land, was struck by lightning and then caught fire. The tree was cut down by the defendant the following day. However, he did not take any further action to stop the fire from spreading, being content simply to allow the fire to burn itself out. Several days later, the weather changed. The wind became stronger and the air temperature increased. The fire revived and spread over the plaintiff's land which was damaged. It was held that the defendant was liable for the damage in that he had failed to remove the nuisance in question from his land. In coming to its decision the Privy Council was of the view that in determining liability for nuisance, no distinction should be drawn between man-made nuisances and natural nuisances. Furthermore, as far as the facts of the case were concerned, there was no substantive difference between the law of nuisance and the law of negligence. In deciding whether the defendant was liable, one should take into account the defendant's knowledge of the hazard as well as his ability to foresee the consequences of not checking or removing it and, also, his ability to abate the nuisance. Importantly, the Privy Council held that in determining whether the defendant had failed to attain the standard of care which the law demanded of him, one should adopt a subjective approach. One would, therefore, take into account the resources of the defendant. One would expect less on the part of an occupier of small premises than from one of a larger property. Similarly, less would be demanded of the infirm than of the able-bodied.

The last in the trilogy of cases is *Leakey v National Trust for Places of Historic or Natural Beauty* (1980). In that case, the claimant owned houses which were situated at the base of a steep conical hill which was owned and occupied by the defendant. Part of the side of the hill which adjoined the claimants' land became unstable. This state of affairs was made known to the defendant by the claimants. However, no remedial action was taken by the defendant. A few weeks later there was a substantial fall of earth and tree stumps from the hill on to the claimant's land. The claimants brought an action in nuisance. The Court of Appeal held the defendant liable. The Court followed *Goldman* and, therefore, refused to draw a distinction between an adverse state of affairs which had been foisted on the defendant by man-made activities and one which arose by way of the operation of nature.

Of fundamental importance is whether *Sedleigh-Denfield, Goldman* and *Leakey* are applicable to Scots law. There is little authority on this point. However, given the need for the pursuer to prove *culpa* on the part of the defender, it is difficult to imagine circumstances where liability could not be imposed in terms of the law of nuisance in Scotland but, on the other hand, fall to be imposed in terms of the law as enunciated in *Sedleigh-Denfield Goldman* and *Leakey*. In other words, it is suggested that the concept of *culpa* in terms of Scots law is probably wider than the degree of fault which is necessary to ground liability for failure to abate a nuisance in English law, as set out in the above trilogy of cases.

(3) A landlord is not liable for every nuisance which emanates from the premises which he has leased (*Smith* v *Scott* (1973)). Rather, a landlord is liable for a nuisance only if he has either authorised the tenant to create the nuisance, or if the creation of the nuisance is either the certain or a highly probable result of the tenant's occupation of the premises concerned. See also *Cocking* v *Eacott* (2016).

(4) The licensor of the nuisance. The occupier of land may be liable for a nuisance which is created on the premises by his licensee (*White* v *Jameson* (1874)), especially if no attempt is made by the licensor either to abate or to remove the nuisance after he becomes aware of its existence. The leading case on this point is *Webster* v *Lord Advocate* (1984). In that case, the pursuer claimed that the noise from the performance of the Edinburgh Military Tattoo, and also the erection of scaffolding to accommodate seating for it, amounted to a nuisance. It was held irrelevant that the contract between the licensees (the Tattoo Policy Committee) and the Secretary of State for Scotland, as occupier of the Edinburgh Castle esplanade, was liable in nuisance for the noise which was caused by the erection of scaffolding (which was to be used to accommodate seating on the esplanade) since he had licensed the creation of the nuisance. It was held irrelevant that the contract between the licensees, the Tattoo Policy Committee and the Secretary of State contained a "no-nuisance" clause, since no attempt had been made by the latter to monitor, or inspect, the activities of the licensee or to enforce the clause. It is, therefore, possible that a licensor could escape liability in nuisance for the conduct of his licensee if the licensor was capable of and did, indeed, take steps to enforce such a clause.

## DEFENCES

### Statutory authority

The basis of this defence is that if Parliament (either the Westminster or the Scottish Parliament) has sanctioned the state of affairs which constitutes the nuisance, the pursuer has no remedy in law. The defence was most commonly invoked during the course of the 19th century in relation to alleged nuisances from the operation of railways. The case law which was embodied in the railway cases was reviewed and also clarified by the House of Lords in the leading case of *Allen v Gulf Oil Refining Ltd* (1981). In that case a private Act of Parliament authorised a multinational company to acquire land, which was situated in a rural area, to construct an oil refinery. However, soon after the refinery commenced operations, residents who lived in the vicinity began to complain about the smell, noise and vibration which emanated from the plant. The House of Lords held that the Act had, by necessary implication, authorised both the construction and also the operation of the refinery, the inevitable consequence of which was the creation of the nuisance in question. The claimants, therefore, failed in their action.

However, the defence of statutory authority does not apply if the relevant activities are carried out negligently. Furthermore, if the relevant statute authorises the relevant activity to be carried out without causing a nuisance, the defence of statutory authority is inapplicable if the activity is carried on in such a manner as to cause a nuisance: *Metropolitan Asylum District Managers v Hill* (1881).

## Prescription

The basic rule here is that the law will not give a remedy in favour of the pursuer who has failed to complain for 20 years or more in the face of a nuisance (*Duncan v Earl of Moray* (1809)). In order for the defence to succeed, the nuisance must have remained substantially constant over the prescriptive period and also have been an actionable nuisance over that period (*Sturges v Bridgman* (1879)). Also, the pursuer must have had either actual or constructive knowledge of the nuisance (*Liverpool Corporation v Coghill and Son* (1918)). The prescriptive period begins when the pursuer could have raised a successful action against the defender. However, even if the defender does acquire a prescriptive right to continue a nuisance, he does not thereby acquire the right to create another nuisance or to increase the intensity of the state of affairs in respect of which the prescriptive right has been acquired (*Baxendale v MacMurray* (1867)).

## Acquiescence

The pursuer may also lose his right to raise an action in nuisance if he acquiesces in the face of a nuisance. The defence of acquiescence is separate from that of prescription (*Collins v Hamilton* (1837)). For the defence to succeed, there requires to be a clear, unequivocal and positive act on the part of the pursuer which indicates that he has consented to the nuisance in question. The person who is alleged to have acquiesced is required to have had both full knowledge of, and also the power to stop the nuisance in question (*Earl of Kintore* v *Pirie* (1903)). Mere silence in the face of the nuisance is insufficient to ground the defence (*Cowan* v *Kinnaird* (1865)). However, occupation of the land which is affected by the nuisance, coupled with the knowledge of the existence of the nuisance, is capable of raising the presumption that the pursuer has acquiesced (*Colville* v *Middleton* (1817)). Also, the longer the pursuer remains impassive in the face of the nuisance, the stronger is the presumption that he has acquiesced in its face. Importantly, it must also be shown that the works, whence the nuisance arises, have been erected at great expense or, alternately, that the works cannot be undone (*Muirhead* v *Glasgow Highland Society* (1864)). It must be stated that this aspect of the law of acquiescence is a grey area of law on which there is little 20th-century authority.

Finally, if the court decides that the pursuer has acquiesced in the face of a nuisance, his successors in title are also denied a remedy. That is to say, the defence of acquiescence runs with the land which is affected by the nuisance.

## REMEDIES

The pursuer requires to have a proprietary interest in the land which is affected by the relevant nuisance before he can raise an action. It is insufficient that the person concerned simply resides in the premises concerned (*Hunter* v *Canary Wharf Ltd* (1997).

The remedies of damages, interdict and declarator, which apply generally in Scots law, apply to the law of nuisance.

### Essential Facts

- The law of nuisance protects the enjoyment of the occupier of land from unreasonable interference which takes place outside that land.
- The courts take a variety of factors into account when determining whether a nuisance exists, namely the social utility of the defender's conduct, the motive of the defender, the nature of the locality, duration and intensity, time of day, sensitivity of pursuer and social utility of thing interfered with.
- Normally, there will require to be some form of emanation from the defender's premises.
- The pursuer requires to prove *culpa* or fault on the part of the defender.

- The author of the nuisance is liable.
- The occupier of the land from which the nuisance emanates is liable.
- A landlord is not liable for every nuisance which emanates from the premises which he has leased.
- The licensor of the relevant nuisance may be liable.
- If Parliament has sanctioned the very state of affairs which constitutes the nuisance, that is a complete defence in a nuisance action.
- The law will not give a remedy in favour of a pursuer who has failed to complain for 20 years or more in the face of a nuisance.
- The pursuer may also lose his right to raise an action in nuisance if he acquiesces in the face of it.
- In order to raise an action in nuisance the pursuer requires to have an interest in the land which is affected by the relevant nuisance.
- The remedies of damages, interdict and declarator are applicable in the law of nuisance.

## Essential Cases

**Watt v Jamieson (1954)**: the law must strike a balance between the right of the proprietor of land to do as he pleases on that land and the right of his neighbour not to be adversely affected by what the former does on his land. Whether an adverse state of affairs ranks as a nuisance is a question of fact and degree. In order to ascertain whether a given state of affairs ranks as a nuisance, one approaches the issue from the viewpoint of the pursuer.

**Kennedy v Glenbelle Ltd (1996)**: in Scots law it is essential that the pursuer proves *culpa* or blame on the part of the defender. The concept of *culpa* is wider than that of negligence.

# 4 OCCUPIER'S LIABILITY

Land may become dangerous by virtue of its physical state. For example, a field which is located in an area where mining took place may contain several deep pits which have been caused by subsidence. Land may also present a danger to the public by virtue of an activity which takes place on the land. For example, a field may be crossed by a railway line or electricity pylons, both of which could present a potential danger to those who visit the field.

By the end of the 19th century it had been established that the occupier of land owed a duty of care in certain circumstances to those who visited the land. However, the law was very complicated and remained so until it was reformed by the Occupiers' Liability (Scotland) Act 1960. The Act varies the rules of the common law in determining the duty of care occupiers of land or other premises are required to take by virtue of their occupation or control of premises, in relation to dangers which are posed due to the state of premises: s 1. It should be noted that the authority of case law decided prior to the passing of the Act is not negated. Indeed, s 1 goes on to provide that the Act does not alter the common law rules which determine the person by whom a duty to show care is owed (ie who occupies the relevant land in the eye of the law). The scope of the Act is not confined to those who occupy land (ie heritable property). Rather, it extends to those who occupy or have control of any fixed or moveable structure, including any vessel, vehicle or aircraft. However, the Act does not apply to roads, streets etc: *Lamont* v *Monklands DC* (1992).

There can be more than one occupier of land for the purposes of the Act: *Mallon* v *Spook Erections Ltd* (1993). As far as having the "occupation or control" of premises is concerned, in *Telfer* v *Glasgow DC* (1974) a vacant property was in the course of being sold by the Co-operative Society (Co-op) to Glasgow District Council (GDC). Both the Co-op and GDC were sued in respect of injuries which the pursuer sustained on the premises. It was held that the fact that the Co-op had the keys to the premises and the *de facto* power to exclude others meant that the Co-op occupied the premises for the purposes of the Act. See also *Dawson* v *Page* (2012).

Finally, it is important to note that the Act places a duty of care on occupiers to all persons entering the relevant premises, irrespective of their status. For example, no distinction is drawn in the Act between those who are lawfully on the relevant premises and those who are not.

# WHAT DUTY IS OWED BY THE OCCUPIER?

Section 2(1) of the 1960 Act provides that:

> "The care which an occupier of premises is required, by reason of his occupation or control of the premises, to show towards a person entering thereon in respect of dangers which are due to the state of the premises or to anything done or omitted to be done on them and for which the occupier is in law responsible except in so far as he is entitled to and does extend, restrict or modify or exclude by agreement his obligations towards that person, be such care as in all the circumstances of the case is reasonable to see that that person will not suffer injury or damage by reason of any such danger."

## Dangers due to the state of the premises

The expression "due to the state of the premises" covers a wide variety of situations, such as dangers which arise from the dilapidated state of the premises to slippery floors, dry rot and poisonous berries: *Taylor* v *Glasgow Corporation* (1922). It should be emphasised that liability stems from the state of the relevant premises, in contradistinction to what the pursuer wishes to do on the premises. This point was emphasised in *Lewis* v *National Assembly of Wales* (2008). There, the claimant (L), who was 14 at the time, was injured while riding a motorcycle on land which was owned and occupied by the defendant. The land had been used by motorcyclists for some years without objection from the Assembly. The land in question comprised a straight stretch of disused single carriageway which ended with a bund about 1 metre high. Behind the bund there was a wide ditch. L was injured as he attempted to negotiate the bund and the ditch. He claimed that the land was inherently dangerous. It was held that his injury was not caused by the state of the premises but, rather, by the use which L chose to make of the premises.

## Reasonable in the circumstances

The occupier is required to do only that which is reasonable in the circumstances. For example, in *McGlone* v *British Railways Board* (1966) a boy, aged 12, climbed up an electricity transformer which belonged to the British Railways Board. The transformer was surrounded on three sides by a large fence and on the other side by a railway. Furthermore, the gap between the fence and the wall was restricted by a barbed wire fan. There were also signs which said "Danger – overhead live wires". The boy was badly burned as a result of an electric shock which he sustained when he came into contact with the wires, high up in the transformer. It was held that the pursuer failed in his action, since the defenders had done all that one could reasonably have demanded of them in the circumstances. Lord Pearce stated (at 12): "In a case like this an occupier does, in my view, act reasonably if he erects an obstacle which a boy must take some trouble to overcome."

It thus becomes a question of degree, to be decided in the light of common sense, how formidable the obstruction must be in a particular case. For example, in *Adams* v *Southern Electricity Board* (1993) a boy aged 15 was electrocuted after he had climbed a pole-mounted high-voltage electrical installation. He was able to do so because the relevant anti-climbing device was in a defective condition. It was held by the Court of Appeal that the Board owed him a duty of care to ensure that he was effectively prevented from climbing the pole.

In *Titchener* v *BRB* (1984) the pursuer, a girl aged 15, was struck by a train while on a busy railway line. The pursuer alleged that the Board was under a duty to maintain the fence which protected the railway line in such a condition as to prevent access to the railway line. The House of Lords held that the duty which was owed by the Board under s 2(1) of the 1960 Act was towards the particular person who entered the premises in question. Since the girl was well aware of the danger from the trains, she was deemed to have been *volenti*, that is, she was deemed to have consented or agreed to run the risk of being injured (see later notes). According to Lord Fraser (at 195):

> "The existence and the extent of a duty to fence will depend on all the facts of the case, including the age and intelligence of the particular person entering the premises. The duty will tend to be higher in a question with a very young or very old person than in the question with a normally active and intelligent adult or adolescent."

Lord Fraser went on to state that the nature of the *locus* in question was also important. He also stated that possibly, if the train which hit the pursuer had been driven negligently, the defence of *volenti non fit iniuria* would not have been applicable.

In *Telfer* v *Glasgow Corporation* (1974) the pursuer (aged 10) fell through the roof of a derelict building which was situated in a working-class area. A large number of children played there. Indeed, it was a glorified playground. It was held that the defender was in breach of s 2 of the Act, on the ground that reasonable attempts should have been made to keep the premises secure. However, the pursuer was held to be 50 per cent contributorily negligent.

If the nature of the premises constitutes an allurement or entrapment to the young it is incumbent on the defender to take the relevant prophylactic measures. This point is illustrated in the sheriff court case of *Morton* v *Glasgow City Council* (2007). In that case the pursuer entered a plot of ground by means of an unlocked gate in which a block of tenement houses were situated and around which the defenders had erected scaffolding. The pursuer (then aged 14) climbed up the scaffolding and fell to the ground, thereby injuring himself. The sheriff held that since the presence of the scaffolding constituted an allurement to young persons, effective measures ought to have been taken to protect them from associated dangers.

*Hill* v *Lovett* (1992) provides an interesting example of the application of the Act. Here, a veterinary surgeon's receptionist was given permission by her employer to enter a private garden (which belonged to her employer) for the purpose of cleaning surgery windows. While in the garden she was bitten on the leg by a dog which was owned by her employer. The bite, which was ostensibly fairly minor in nature, had, ultimately, disastrous consequences. It was held that her employer, the occupier of the garden, owed her a duty of care in law.

Liability under the Act also extends to the failure on the part of the occupier to take into account the reasonably foreseeable actions of others. In *Hosie* v *Arbroath FC* (1978) football fans deliberately pushed down a gate (which was in a potentially dangerous condition) in the defender's stadium, in order to gain access to it. Unfortunately, the gate fell on and crushed the pursuer, who was severely injured. It was held that the defender was liable under the Act since the actions of the fans were reasonably foreseeable.

The defender need not provide protection against obvious danger on his land which arises from a natural feature such as a lake or a cliff: *Tomlinson* v *Congleton Borough Council* (2004). See also *Fegan* v *Highland Regional Council* (2007) and *Leonard* v *Loch Lomond and the Trossachs National Park Authority* (2014). *Evans* v *Kosmar Villa Holidays* (2007) is authority for the proposition that there is no duty to protect the pursuer against obvious dangers whether natural or man-made. See also *Grimes* v *Hawkins* (2011) and *Dawson* v *Page* (2012). Whereas a danger, whether man-made or natural, may be obvious during the day, the danger may not be apparent during the night. This point is illustrated in the Outer House case of *Cowan* v *The Hopetoun House Preservation Trust* (2013). In that case, the pursuer was injured when he fell into the ha-ha (a ditch or vertical drop) on the land which was occupied by the defender. The accident occurred at night, when the pursuer was returning to a carpark after participating in a guided walk to observe bats. It was held that the ha-ha was an unusual feature, by virtue of its concealed nature, particularly in the dark, and therefore constituted a danger due to the state of the premises, for the purposes of s 2(1) of the Act.

Finally, the relevant precautions which the defender requires to take in order to avoid liability under the Act must be commensurate with the risk which is posed to the person who enters the land. In other words, there is no need for the occupier to guard against risks which are negligible (see, for example, *Phee* v *Gordon* (2013)).

## LANDLORD'S LIABILITY

Section 3 of the 1960 Act places on a landlord a duty of care, in respect of parts of premises which have been leased, similar that pertaining to an occupier of premises, in a situation under which the landlord is responsible for either the maintenance or repair of the premises.

## DEFENCE

Section 2(3) of the 1960 Act preserves the defence of *volenti non fit iniuria,* that is to say that there is no liability if the pursuer has fully and freely consented to run the risk to which he has been exposed.

---

### Essential Facts

- The Occupiers' Liability (Scotland) Act 1960 varies the rules of common law governing occupier's liability.
- The duty which an occupier of land owes in respect of dangers which are due to the state of the premises is such as is reasonable in all the circumstances.
- Landlords owe certain duties under the Act.
- The defence of *volenti non fit iniuria* applies.

**Essential Cases**

**McGlone v BRB (1966)**: occupier only required to do that which is reasonable in the circumstances.

**Titchener v BRB (1984)**: extent of duty which is owed under the Act is towards particular person who enters the premises depends on all facts of the case including the age and intelligence of the particular person entering the premises.

# 5 PRODUCT LIABILITY

Sometimes the products which we buy are defective. In the vast majority of cases such defects result in the consumer simply returning the product to the retailer. Occasionally, however, such defects may cause injury to the consumer or his property. For example, I may eat a piece of cake and cut my mouth while eating it, because the manufacturer has negligently allowed a nail to enter a mixing vat when the cake is being made. Again, I could buy a washing machine which has a defective motor, the upshot of which is that the machine catches fire and damages my kitchen.

Until fairly recently, one could only obtain redress as far as the law of delict was concerned by invoking the common law of negligence. However, in order to invoke the law of negligence successfully, one requires to prove that the manufacturer of the product failed to attain the standard of care which the law demanded of him. In practice this may be difficult. Such difficulty prompted the EU to introduce a legal regime (Council Directive on Liability for Defective Products, No 85/374/EEC, which was transposed into UK law) which was based on strict liability, thereby rendering it unnecessary for someone who was injured by a defective product, to prove negligence.

We look first at how the common law addresses harm which is caused by defective products, and, second, at how liability is dealt with under statute.

## LIABILITY UNDER THE COMMON LAW

Liability in relation to liability for defective products was reviewed in the leading case of *Donoghue* v *Stevenson* (1932). In that case, the pursuer, Mrs Donoghue, claimed that she had entered a café in Paisley with her friend. Her friend purchased a bottle of ginger beer (which had been manufactured by the defender) for her consumption. She drank some of the ginger beer, but as more of it was poured into her glass, the remains of a snail came out of the bottle. She alleged that she suffered both shock, and also severe gastro-enteritis, as a result. The House of Lords, by a majority, held that the manufacturer owed Mrs Donoghue a duty of care in the law of negligence. Lord Atkin, in enunciating the so-called "narrow rule" in the case, stated:

> "a *manufacturer* of products which he sells in such a form as to show that he intends them to reach the *ultimate consumer* in the form in which they

left him with no *reasonable possibility of intermediate examination* and with knowledge that the absence of reasonable care in the *preparation or putting up of the products* will result in an injury to the *consumer's life or property* owes a duty of care to the *consumer to take that reasonable care*" (emphasis added).

## The extension of the narrow rule in *Donoghue* v *Stevenson*

The narrow rule has been extended by the courts over the years. We shall now see how this has been done.

### Liability of manufacturers

Manufacturer's liability has been extended widely to include those who repair and supply products (*Herschal* v *Stewart and Ardern Ltd* (1940)); fitters (*Malfroot* v *Noxal Ltd* (1935)); the erectors of tombstones (*Brown* v *Cotterill* (1934)); the installers of electrical equipment (*Eccles* v *Cross and McIlwham* (1938)); local authorities which supply water (*Barnes* v *Irwell Valley Water Board* (1939)); and vendors of motor vehicles (*Andrews* v *Hopkinson* (1957)).

The product itself need not have been manufactured negligently. It may have been rendered dangerous for the consumer to use in the absence of instructions and warnings (*Webber* v *McCausland* (1948)).

### Ultimate consumer

The courts have extended the expression "ultimate consumer" to include the ultimate user of the article (*Grant* v *Australian Knitting Mills* (1936)); anyone into whose hands the article might pass (*Barnett* v *Packer* (1940)); and also anyone who is in close proximity to the article in question (*Brown* v *Cotterill* (1934)).

### Sale

The product in question does not need to be sold in order for liability to lie (*Hawkins* v *Coulsdon and Purley UDC* (1954)).

### Intermediate examination

In *Donoghue* v *Stevenson* (1932) Lord Atkin stated that the liability of manufacturers depended on there being no reasonable possibility of intermediate examination. However, the courts have subsequently adopted a different approach. "Possibility" now should be interpreted as "probability" (*Haseldine* v *C A Daw* (1941)).

### Preparation and design

In addition to obvious defects, such as the extraneous matter which is contained in the product in question, the relevant defect may consist of a defect in design (*Hindustan SS Co* v *Siemens Bros and Co Ltd* (1955)); an inadequacy in the container of the product in question (*Bates* v *Batey* (1913)); and also the inadequacy of a label on the container, or an advert which pertains to the product which fails to warn of the dangers of the product (*Buchan* v *Ortho Pharmaceutical (Canada) Ltd* v *North America Cyanamid Ltd* (1958)).

## Consumer's life or property

The defender will be liable in relation to a product defect which causes the person who either uses or consumes the product, to become ill (*Donoghue* v *Stevenson* (1932)) or injured (*Brown* v *Cotterill* (1934)).

## Owes a duty ... to take that reasonable care

It is the latency of the defect, in contrast to the potential harm which is posed by the product, which is covered by the narrow rule. In *McTear* v *Imperial Tobacco Ltd* (2005) the pursuer claimed that her deceased husband had died from lung cancer which had been caused by his consuming cigarettes manufactured by the defenders. It was held in the Outer House that the cigarettes in question were not defective products within the meaning of the narrow rule in *Donoghue* v *Stevenson* (1932) because the cigarettes did not contain some extraneous substance as a result of manufacturing error. In effect, the defender intended to manufacture the cigarettes in the very form and state in which they reached the deceased. The latter, in turn, received the very product which he wished to purchase, and proceeded to consume it in the manner in which cigarettes are intended to be consumed. Furthermore, the cigarettes met public expectation. In the last analysis, the cigarettes could not be said to be defective.

In some circumstances the manufacturer is under a duty to warn the consumer of a danger which is associated with the product. It is a question of fact and degree, in every case, whether a manufacturer has given sufficient warning (*Re Children's Drink* (1993)) in relation to the dangers which any particular product may pose to the consumer (*Lewis* v *University of Bristol* (1999)).

However, the duty to warn arises only if there is a foreseeable risk that the consumer will be led to believe that something is safe when it is not. Provided that the ordinary consumer is in a position to make an informed choice, there is no duty to warn of any dangers which are associated with the use of the product (*McTear* v *Imperial Tobacco Ltd* (2005)). There is no duty to warn of risks of which it would be reasonable to expect an ordinary consumer to be aware. For example in *McTear* the pursuer averred that the defenders owed her late husband a duty of care to warn him of the dangers which were associated with smoking. It was held that since the products in question carried no hidden danger, the defenders were not under a duty to give any warnings about the product. Furthermore, the public awareness that smoking was linked with health risks and, in particular lung cancer, was so widespread that the defenders had no duty to give warnings about it.

## LIABILITY UNDER THE CONSUMER PROTECTION ACT 1987

### What is a "product"?

The 1987 Act defines the expression "product" widely. A product is defined as any goods or electricity, and includes a product which is comprised in another product, whether by virtue of being a component part or raw material, or otherwise (s 1(2)). Therefore, in a complex product such as a television, a defective "chip" would rank as a product, as well as the television itself.

### Liability under the Act

Under s 2(1) of the 1987 Act it is provided that where any damage is caused wholly or partly by a defect in a product the following persons are liable for the damage:

(a) the producer of the product;

(b) any person who, by putting his name on the product or using a trade mark or other distinguishing mark in relation to the product, has held himself out to be the producer of the product;

(c) any person who has imported the product into a Member State from a place outside the Member States in order, in the course of any business of his, to supply it to another.

Liability under the statute is strict but not absolute (*A* v *National Blood Authority* (2001)). In sharp contrast to the position under the common law, there is no need for the pursuer to prove negligence.

### *Producers*

The expression "producer" of the product is defined in s 1(2) as:

(a) the person who manufactured it;

(b) in the case of a substance which has not been manufactured but has been won or abstracted, the person who won or abstracted it;

(c) in the case of a product which has not been manufactured, won or abstracted, but essential characteristics of which are attributable to an industrial or other process which has been carried out (for example, in relation to agricultural produce) the person who carried out that process.

Paragraph (a) needs little comment. As far as paragraph (b) is concerned, examples would include a mining company which abstracted coal from an opencast mine or those who abstract mineral water from an underground source. Such individuals would rank as producers, and would be liable for any relevant defects in the product.

Under paragraph (c) a fish curer, for example, would be liable for any harmful preservatives which are used in smoking fish. However, it is not necessary that the relevant defect derives from the process in question: for example, the fish curer would be liable for injury which is caused by a fishing hook which is embedded in the flesh of the fish.

### "Those holding themselves out as producers"

The rationale of making those who hold themselves out as producers is that consumers tend to rely on the reputation of certain companies and organisations. It is the very act of those who hold themselves out as producers which makes them liable under the Act. Therefore, it is quite irrelevant whether consumers were under the impression that a so-called "own-brander" actually produced the product.

### "Importers"

Any person who imports a product into a Member State from a place which is outside the EU is also liable. Therefore, even if the non-EU producer cannot be sued, the importer of the product into the EU can be.

### Liability of suppliers

Primarily liability for defective products lies with the producer. However, it may be difficult at times to identify the producer. Therefore, the 1987 Act provides that where any damage is caused wholly or partly by a defect in the product, any person who supplied the product is liable if the person who suffered the damage requests the supplier to identify the producer, "own-brander" or importer, and the supplier fails to comply with the request within a reasonable period (s 2(3)).

### Meaning of "defect"

There is a defect in a product if the safety of the product is not such as persons are entitled to expect, and for those purposes "safety" in relation to a product includes safety with respect to products comprised in that product and safety in the context of risks of damage to property, as well as in the context of risks of death or personal injury (s 3(1)). In determining what persons generally are entitled to expect in relation to a product, all circumstances are required to be taken into account, including:

(a) the manner in which, and purposes for which, the product has been marketed, its get up, the use of any mark in relation to the product and any instructions for, or warnings with respect to, doing or refraining from doing anything with or in relation to the product;

(b) what may reasonably be expected to be done with or in relation to the product;

(c) the time when the product was supplied by its producer to another (s 3(2)).

The test as to whether the product is defective is objective (*Worsley* v *Tambrands Ltd* (2000)). The pursuer requires to prove, on a balance of probabilities, that the product is defective (*Foster* v *Biosil* (2001)). While there is no need for the pursuer to establish fault on the part of the defender, the pursuer must show that the relevant injury, or damage, was caused by the defect in question (*Richardson* v *LRC Products Ltd* (2000)). However, a product is not defective because its common attributes are such that a risk of injury is posed to persons who use such items improperly (*A* v *National Blood Authority* (2001)). For example, it has been held that a disposable cup which contains a hot beverage, which was securely covered by a lid that could, nonetheless, be dislodged if the cup fell and struck a hard surface was not a defective product: since people generally know that if a hot drink is spilled, a serious injury may result. The risk was obvious (*B* v *McDonald's Restaurants Ltd* (2002)). It should be noted that the safety of the product in question is what the public, in general, are *entitled* to expect, in contrast to what the public *actually* expect. The test is objective. In the last analysis, the court decides what the public is entitled to expect (*A* v *National Blood Authority* (2001)). The court decides whether that expectation is fulfilled in respect of the actual product which has injured the pursuer, as opposed to potential defectiveness of products of that genus or type. In determining what the public can legitimately expect, appropriate warnings can be taken into account (*Worsley* v *Tambrands Ltd* (2000)).

Since liability under the Act is strict, it is irrelevant that the defect in question could have been avoided by the defender (*A* v *National Blood Authority* (2001)).

The European Court of Justice has decided that where it is found that products which belong to the same group, or form part of the same production series, have a potential defect, it is possible to classify such a product of that group as defective without there being any need to establish that the product in question is defective (*Boston Scientific Medizintechnik GmbH* v *AOK Sachsen-Anhalt-Die Gesundheitskasse* (2013)).

In deciding whether a product is defective, the nature of the potential injury is also relevant. If the product can pose a potential threat to delicate parts of the body, such as the eye, appropriate measures require to be taken (*Abouzaid* v *Mothercare Ltd* (2001)). The Act requires the court to take into account what may reasonably be expected to be done with or in relation to the product (s 3(2)(b)). For example, the fact that a person cuts his mouth with a sharp knife while eating a piece of meat does not render the knife defective in terms of the Act, since it is not expected that a person will put a sharp knife in his mouth. In deciding what may reasonably may be expected to be done with the product, account should be taken of possible misuse by children, the elderly and the disabled, in contrast to the reasonable person.

## Defences

### (1) Compliance with legal requirement

It is a defence for the defender to prove that the defect in question is attributable to compliance with any requirement which is imposed by or under any enactment or with any Community obligation (s 4(1)(a)).

### (2) That the defender did not supply the product in question

It is a defence that the defender did not supply the product to another (s 4(1)(b)). Section 46 of the Act defines the expression "supply" broadly and includes the selling, hiring out or lending of the goods and giving the goods as a prize or otherwise making a gift of the goods.

### (3) Non-commercial supply of the product

It is a defence that the only supply of the product to another by the defender was otherwise than in the course of a business (s 4(1)(c)).

### (4) Subsequent defect

It is a defence that the defect did not exist in the product at the relevant time (s 4(1)(d)). Importantly, in relation to producers, own-branders and importers the relevant time is the time when the product was supplied by them (s 4(2)(a)). In relation to the liability of others (for example, retailers) the relevant time is the time when the product was last supplied by a producer, own-brander or importer (s 4(2)(b)).

## (5) State of knowledge

It is a defence that the state of scientific and technical knowledge at the relevant time was not such that a producer of products of the same description as the product in question might be expected to have discovered the defect if it had existed in his products while they were under his control (s 4(1)(e)). The defence is commonly known as the "development risk" defence.

The state of knowledge must be construed so as to include all data in the information circuit of the scientific community as a whole, bearing in mind, in the context of a reasonableness test, the actual opportunities for the information to circulate (*A* v *National Blood Authority* (2001)). The defence is not concerned with the conduct or knowledge of individual producers. The test is objective (*Commission of European Communities v UK* (1997)) and includes constructive knowledge, that is to say what the producer *ought* to know. The relevant time to assess the state of knowledge is the time when the product was put into circulation (*A* v *National Blood Authority* (2001)).

## Defect in subsequent product

It is a defence if the defect in the product consisted of a defect in a product (the subsequent product) in which the product had been comprised and was wholly attributable to the design of the subsequent product, or to compliance by the producer of the product in question with instructions given by the producer of the subsequent product (s 4(1)(f)).

## For what is the defender liable under the Act?

The defender is liable for damage which is caused wholly or partly by a defect in a product (s 2(1)). "Damage" is defined as death or personal injury or any loss of or damage to any property including land (s 5(1)). Pure economic loss is not recoverable. There is no liability in respect of damage which is caused to the product itself, or for the loss of or any damage to the whole or part of any product which has been supplied with the relevant product comprised in it (s 5(2)). Furthermore, there is no liability in respect of loss of or damage to any property which at the time it is lost or damaged is not:

(a) of a description of property ordinarily intended for private use, occupation or consumption; and

(b) intended by the person suffering the loss or damage mainly for his own private use, occupation or consumption (s 5(3)).

Damage which is inflicted to commercial property is, therefore, not actionable. No damages can be awarded in relation to loss or damage to property if the loss or damage does not exceed £275 (s 5(4)).

It is important to note that *any* person who has suffered actionable damage can raise an action under the Act. For example, a visitor to my house could recover damages in respect of any injury which he receives from a defective television exploding in my lounge. Finally, liability under the Act cannot be excluded by any contract term, by any notice or by any other provision (s 7).

## Essential Facts

- One can recover damages for defective products under the common law in terms of the narrow rule in *Donoghue* v *Stevenson* (1932).
- The rule has been expanded over the years.
- The main disadvantage with the common law is that it is often difficult to prove that the defender was negligent. Such difficulty was brought to a head by the Thalidomide tragedy.
- Pt 1 of the Consumer Protection Act 1987 introduces a regime based on strict liability for dangerous products.
- The Act gives the term "product" a wide definition.
- Liability largely falls on the producer.
- A product is defective if the safety of the product is not such as persons generally are entitled to expect.
- The test as to whether the product is defective is objective.
- It is irrelevant that the defect in question could have been avoided by the defender.
- The statute contains a number of defences, the most important and controversial being the "state of the art" defence.
- The defender is liable for damage which is caused wholly or partly by a defect in a product.
- Damage to commercial property is not actionable.
- No damages can be awarded in relation to loss or damage which does not exceed £275.

# 6 DEFAMATION

The vast majority of delict cases consist of the defender inflicting some form of physical harm on the pursuer or his property. However, in certain cases the type of harm or interest which is protected by the law of delict is more subtle in nature. This chapter concerns the protection of the pursuer's reputation. The law of defamation has two essential purposes. The first is to enable the individual to protect his reputation. The second is to preserve the right of free speech. These two purposes necessarily conflict.

## PUBLICATION

In contrast to the law of England, the publication of a defamatory statement to a third party is not necessary in Scotland in order for liability to lie. In *Stuart v Moss* (1885) a theatre manager, Moss, engaged an actor, who was called Stuart, to perform in three towns. However, the actor failed to live up to Moss's expectation. Moss wrote to Stuart: "You advertise what you are not capable of." The words were written to Stuart alone. It was held that Moss was liable. The reason why Scots law allows the pursuer to recover for words which are published to him alone is that the Scots law of defamation derives from the *actio iniuriarum* in Roman law which allowed one to recover simply in respect of injury to one's feelings. In contrast, the basis of the English law of defamation is the protection of the claimant's reputation. Therefore, in England it is necessary that the defamatory statement is published to others. Again, in contrast to English law, there is no distinction in Scots law between words which are spoken (slander) and words which are written (libel). The general rule is that the person who circulates a defamatory statement, for example a publisher, printer or newsagent, is equally liable in terms of the law of defamation with the author of the statement (*Wright and Greig v Outram* (1890)). Similarly, a person who simply repeats a defamatory statement is liable, in addition to the maker of the original statement (*MacDonald v Martin* (1935)).

A person who simply allows defamatory matter to remain in existence after he becomes aware of its existence, may be liable in defamation. For example, in the Court of Appeal case of *Byrne v Deane* (1937) it was held that the defendant golf club had published a notice which had been written by an unknown person, which was alleged to have been defamatory of the claimant, simply by allowing the notice to remain on the club notice board after the defendant had become aware of its existence. *Byrne* was followed by the Court of Appeal in *Tamiz* v *Google* (2013). In that case, the defendant had allowed a blog to remain on its web platform after the claimant had notified the defendant that he was of the opinion that the blog was defamatory of him. The court held that if it were found that the defendant had allowed defamatory material to remain on its platform after it had been notified of its presence, and had had reasonable time within which to remove it, it could be inferred to have associated itself with or to have made itself responsible for the continued presence of the material, and thus become a publisher of the material.

## WHAT IS DEFAMATORY?

In *Sim* v *Stretch* (1936), in attempting to formulate a working definition of what defamation means in law, Lord Atkin stated: "would the words tend to lower the plaintiff in the estimation of right-thinking members of society generally?". As far as the Faulks Report of 1972 was concerned, words would rank as defamatory if the words would be likely to affect persons adversely in the estimation of reasonable people generally. Generally, a defamatory statement involves some imputation against the character or reputation of the pursuer, including his business or financial reputation. The notion of lowering the reputation of the pursuer in the minds of others is a common theme.

It is a question of law as to whether the particular words are defamatory: *Gordon* v *John Leng* (1919).

Examples of what has been held to rank as defamatory include the following:

### Dishonesty

It is defamatory to allege that someone is a thief, crook or swindler etc: *Harkness* v *Daily Record* (1924).

### Sexual immorality etc

In *Morrison* v *Ritchie* (1902) a false birth notice was inserted in a newspaper to the effect that a child had been born to the pursuer and his wife a month after they had married. This was held to be defamatory. However, the case could be decided differently today, given the fact that unmarried couples living together is much more acceptable now than when *Morrison* was decided.

At one time, to allege that the pursuer was homosexual was clearly defamatory: *AB* v *XY* (1917). However, it may not be so today: *Quilty* v *Windsor* (1999). Similarly, an imputation of illegitimacy has been held to be defamatory in the English case of *Solomon* v *Simmons* (1954). It is doubtful whether this decision would be followed by a Scottish court today. Similarly, in the leading case of *Youssoupoff* v *Metro-Goldwyn-Mayer* (1934) it was held defamatory to say that a woman had been raped. While this case has never been overruled, it may not represent the modern law.

## Improper, disgraceful or dishonourable conduct

In *McLaren* v *Robertson* (1859) it was held defamatory to allege that the pursuer was "The Greatest Liar in the World". In *McFarlane* v *Black* (1886–87) the defender contended that the pursuer, who was a parliamentary candidate, sneered at Divine Government. It was held that the jury were entitled to hold that the words were defamatory. Again, in *Cuthbert* v *Linklater* (1936) Wendy Wood, who was a prominent Scottish Nationalist, raised an action against the author Eric Linklater. In Linklater's novel Beaty Bracken removes a Union Jack from Stirling Castle and places it in a public urinal. In fact, in 1932 Wendy Wood had removed a Union Jack from Stirling Castle and thrown it to a guard. It was held defamatory to impute such conduct to the pursuer. In *Gordon* v *John Leng and Co* (1919) a newspaper article alleged that the pursuer, a colonel, had ordered his men to surrender. This was held to be defamatory. Finally, in *Monson* v *Tussauds Ltd* (1894) it was held defamatory to impute that the claimant had committed murder.

## Unfitness for occupation or profession

In *MacKellar* v *Duke of Sutherland* (1859) it was held defamatory to state that a minister was incompetent in office. Also in *McRostie* v *Ironside* (1849) it was held defamatory for the defender to state that the pursuer carried on lawsuits for the purpose of creating money for himself, in the wanton disregard of the interests of clients.

## Insolvency and uncreditworthiness

To allege that the pursuer is insolvent or financially uncreditworthy is defamatory. In *Russell* v *Stubbs* (1913) it was falsely alleged that a decree in absence had been pronounced against the pursuer. It was held that this was defamatory. Again, in *AB* v *CD* (1904) the defender claimed that the pursuer, who was a solicitor, had been "cleaned out and lost his all"; this was held to be defamatory.

## Unsoundness of mind

To impute unsoundness of mind is defamatory: *MacKintosh* v *Weir* (1875).

## Loathsome disease

In *A* v *B* (1907) it was held defamatory to state that the pursuer was suffering from venereal disease. In the American case of *Simpson* v *Press Publishing* (1900) it was held defamatory to say that someone was suffering from leprosy. It could possibly be defamatory to say that the pursuer was suffering from AIDS or was HIV positive, even if the relevant statement made it quite clear that the condition was not acquired by way of any form of sexual misconduct on the part of the pursuer.

## OBJECTIVE APPROACH

The courts adopt an objective approach to ascertaining the meaning of words. In other words, the court asks what the words would convey to an ordinary person reading the article in question: *Hunter* v *Ferguson* (1906). The court decides how the ordinary man or woman would analyse the article etc: *Lewis* v *Daily Telegraph* (1964). In order to ascertain whether the article is defamatory the court seeks to attribute to the relevant words a reasonable, natural and necessary meaning: *Russell* v *Stubbs Ltd* (1913). An interesting Scottish case where this point was illustrated was *MacLeod* v *Newsquest (Sunday Herald) Ltd* (2007) which concerned an alleged attack on a journalist by the defender. The item concerned gave an account of a ceremony at which there had been awarded "the prestigious Tartan Bollocks Award which is given to the Holyrood hack who has made the biggest gaffe of the year". The newspaper contained the following passage:

> "Angus MacLeod of the *Times* who, like Alexander Graham Bell, is justly renowned for his powers of invention, came close with his confident prediction that Jim Wallace would still be leading the Lib Dems in 2007. Mr Wallace repaid the faith shown in him by promptly announcing his retirement."

The pursuer complained that the article conveyed to the reader the false impression that he had a reputation for his powers of invention; that he was a disreputable journalist who made up stories, rather than investigated them; that he was not a fit and proper person to be employed by *The Times* or the BBC; and that he had invented a conversation with Mr Wallace. However, the Lord Ordinary (Lord Macphail) held that the words complained of were not defamatory, in that an ordinary reader would simply interpret the words as being written for his entertainment, in a cheerful, irreverent and playful spirit, and had contained elements of fantasy. It was clear from the language which was employed that the article could not be regarded as an attack upon the pursuer, who therefore failed in his action.

The point that the courts adopt an objective approach when ascertaining the meaning of the relevant article was re-emphasised in the Queen's Bench case of *Thour v Royal Free Hampstead NHS Trust* (2012). The court stated that the governing principle as to whether the words could be construed as libellous, was one of reasonableness. In short, one had to ascertain how a hypothetical reasonable reader would construe the article. Such a reader was not naive but, at the same time, not unduly suspicious. He could indulge in a certain amount of loose thinking.

*Charleston v News Group Newspapers Ltd* (1995) is an interesting case which illustrates these points. In that case two soap opera stars sued in respect of material published in the defendant's newspaper which depicted the claimant's faces superimposed upon two near-naked torsos who were engaged in performing a sexual act. The article, which was printed beneath the picture, castigated the makers of the pornographic computer game which had generated the images in question. However, the claimants contended that many readers would simply ignore the article and focus attention on the photograph. The Court of Appeal held that it was necessary to consider both the article and the picture as a whole. In the last analysis, it was held that, taken as a whole, the picture and the article were not capable of being defamatory.

It is possible that if one part of a publication says something which is disreputable of the pursuer but that is removed by the conclusion, the bane and the antidote must be taken together: *Chalmers v Payne* (1835). However, if a publication repeats a defamatory allegation which is made by someone else and then purports to dispel such an allegation, the publication can be deemed not to be defamatory only in the clearest of circumstances: *Jameel* v *Times Newspapers* (2004). In the leading Scottish case of *Wright and Greig* v *George Outram and Co* (1890) Lord Kyllachy stated that:

"If a newspaper gives circulation to a slander, it is simply in the position of any other person circulating a slander, and the general rule is that a person circulating a slander is answerable equally with the author of the slander."

There is, however, an uneasy tension between the so-called "repetition rule", which dictates that a person who simply repeats a defamatory allegation is automatically liable, and the general rule which was enunciated in *Charleston*, to the effect that in order to ascertain whether an article is defamatory the article should be read as a whole. *Robertson* v *Newsquest (Sunday Herald) Ltd* (2006) is authority for the proposition that not only must one look at the article as a whole in order to ascertain the meaning of a publication, one must also look at the article as a whole in order to ascertain whether the defender has repeated a defamatory allegation.

## Innuendo

Words innocent in themselves may bear some secondary defamatory meaning. For example, it may seem quite innocuous for a newspaper to report that X was seen playing football with his children in a public park. However, the words would assume a different hue if it was known that X was a parish priest! The court must examine the statement in the light of the circumstances in which the statement was made or communicated, to ascertain if the words in question bear a secondary meaning. For example, making a waxwork model of a person acquitted of a murder charge might not be defamatory. However, placing a model of the plaintiff beside a room called "The Chamber of Horrors" which contains models of convicted murderers may be defamatory: *Monson* v *Tussauds* (1894). In *Morrison* v *Ritchie* (1902) a newspaper contained an announcement of the engagement of a couple who were already married was held to be an innuendo that they had been living in sin. Again, in *Tolley* v *Fry* (1931) the defendants, who were a firm of chocolate manufacturers, published a caricature of the claimant who was a famous amateur golfer, depicting him playing golf in the company of a caddie who was holding up packets of the defendants' chocolate. A packet of Fry's chocolate protruded from Tolley's pocket. Below the caricature was a limerick in the following terms:

"The caddie to Tolley said, Oh Sir,
Good shot, Sir. That ball, see it go, Sir,
My word how it flies,
Like a cartet of Frys,
They're handy, they're good, and priced low, Sir."

The caricature and the limerick also described the merits of Fry's chocolate. In the last analysis, the whole publication was plainly an advertisement for the defendants' goods.

The claimant did not allege that the advert was defamatory in itself. Rather, he alleged that the advert bore an innuendo to the effect that the he had agreed, or permitted, his portrait to be exhibited for the purpose of the advertisement of the defendants' chocolate, and that he had done so for gain and reward, and had thereby prostituted his reputation as an amateur golfer for advertising purposes. The House of Lords held that the caricature was capable of bearing such an innuendo.

*Cassidy* v *Daily Mirror Newspapers Ltd* (1929) illustrates the same point. Here, the defendants published in a newspaper a photograph of a racehorse owner called Cassidy and a Miss X. Alongside the photograph was an announcement that the couple had just become engaged. However, the claimant was known among her acquaintances as the lawful wife of Cassidy. The defendants were unaware of this fact. Mrs Cassidy successfully claimed that the publication bore an innuendo to the effect that reasonably minded people would have formed the impression that she was not the wife of Cassidy but was living with him in immoral cohabitation.

It is a matter of fact whether the words should be construed in the defamatory sense: *Fairbairn* v *SNP* (1980). However, it is a matter of law to determine whether the words complained of are capable of carrying an innuendo. The court must ascertain whether an innuendo can reasonably be extracted from the language which is used: *Duncan* v *Associated Scottish Newspapers Ltd* (1929).

However, facts which come to light *after* the defamatory words are published cannot be founded upon in an action which is based on an innuendo. The leading case is *Grappelli* v *Derek Block (Holdings) Ltd* (1981). The claimant was a musician of international repute. He employed managers or agents. The defendant arranged for the plaintiff to give concerts at various venues at specified dates. However, bookings were made without the claimant's authority and had to be cancelled. When informing the managers of the various concert halls where the concerts were about to take place about the cancellations, the defendant stated that Grappelli was ill and would never tour again. Later in the year, authentic notices appeared in national newspapers which gave dates of forthcoming concerts on the same dates as the cancelled ones, but in different towns. The claimant brought an action against the defendant on the grounds that a person reading the authentic notices would form the impression that the claimant had given a reason for cancelling the concerts which he knew to be false. The Court of Appeal held that since the cause of action in defamation had to be known as soon as the words which were complained of were published, any extrinsic facts which were relied on to support a legal innuendo had to be known at the time of publication by those to whom they were published. Since no such extrinsic facts were known at the relevant date, the claimant failed in his action. Lord Denning MR emphasised the point that words cannot be made into a cause of action by reason of facts which come to the knowledge of the reader after the article etc is published.

However, if words in an article are defamatory and only the identification of the pursuer is in issue, words in the subsequent article which identify the pursuer can be founded upon in a defamation action: *Hayward* v *Thomson* (1981).

It is sufficient for the pursuer to prove that there are people who might understand the words in a defamatory sense. There is, therefore, no need for the pursuer to adduce evidence that some people did understand the words in such a sense: *Hough* v *London Express Newspaper Ltd* (1940).

### False innuendo

Sometimes the pursuer may allege that the defender has used words which have acquired a meaning which is quite different from their literal or dictionary meaning. In such a case, an innuendo must be pled by the pursuer. To say that someone is "queer" or "gay" can bear quite a different meaning from "peculiar" or "of a happy disposition", respectively. In *Allsop* v *Church of England Newspaper* (1972) a well-known journalist was described as having a "pre-occupation with the bent". This was held to be capable of being defamatory.

### MODE OF COMMUNICATION

The defamatory statement need not be in words. For example, it can take the form of a cartoon (*Tolley* v *Fry* (1931)) or an effigy (*Monson* v *Tussauds* (1894)).

## STATEMENT MUST BE ABOUT A PERSON

The person who is defamed must be living. In other words, one cannot recover damages in relation to defamatory words which solely reflect on the reputation of a dead person. One's reputation dies with one. Furthermore, in *Broom* v *Ritchie* (1904) it was held that slander of a deceased person gives no claim for solatium to his widow or children.

A juristic person, such as a bank, can sue under the law of defamation provided that its professional or commercial reputation is struck at: *North of Scotland Banking Co* v *Duncan* (1857); *South Hetton Coal Co* v *North Eastern News Association* (1894). However, it has been held that a local authority cannot sue in relation to defamatory words which reflect on its governing reputation, since to allow it to do so would impose both substantial and unjustifiable restrictions on freedom of expression: *Derbyshire County Council* v *Times Newspapers* (1992).

## DEFAMATORY WORDS MUST REFER TO THE PURSUER

The words which are complained of must refer to the pursuer. It is an essential cause of an action of defamation that the words which are complained of should be published of the pursuer. Where the pursuer is not named, the test as to whether he is referred to is whether the words would reasonably lead people who are acquainted with the pursuer to the conclusion that he was the person who was referred to: *Knuppfer* v *London Express Newspaper Ltd* (1944). It is irrelevant that the defender did not wish to refer to the pursuer: *Hulton* v *Jones* (1910). The relevant words need not contain a key or pointer to the pursuer: *Morgan* v *Odhams Press Ltd* (1971). Furthermore, it is irrelevant that no-one believed that the relevant words were true. This form of liability may now infringe Art 10 of the ECHR which preserves the right of freedom of expression: *O'Shea* v *MGN Ltd* (2001). The Defamation Act 1996, ss 2–4 inclusive makes provision for an offer of amends etc in relation to innocent defamation.

## DEFAMATION OF A CLASS

The general rule is that if one defames a class of people, this is not actionable. For example, to say that "all lawyers are thieves" is not actionable. However, if the group is small and each individual member of the group can be identified then each member of the group can sue: *Browne* v *Thomson and Co* (1912).

## FALSITY

The pursuer must aver, but need not prove, that the statement is false. If the statement is defamatory, it is presumed to be untrue and the defender must prove that it is true: *Jameel* v *Wall Street Journal* (2005).

## DEFENCES

### *Veritas* (Truth)

It is a complete defence to publish something which is true, no matter how hurtful it is to the pursuer. For example, if a popular newspaper were to report that a professor of law had been fined for drinking strong lager in George Square in Glasgow and this happened to be true, he would have no remedy in the law of defamation. In short, the law will not permit a man to recover damages in respect of injury to character which he does not possess: *McPherson* v *Daniels* (1829). It is irrelevant that the statement is inspired by malice. The literal truth is unnecessary. It is sufficient for the statement to be true in substance. The defender must justify the sting of the charge: *Alexander* v *N E Railway* (1865). Here, a statement in an article that the plaintiff had been convicted of travelling in a train without a ticket and had been fined £1 with 3 weeks' imprisonment in default of payment was capable of being justified by proof that he had, indeed, been convicted of the offence but the offence carried only 2 weeks' imprisonment. Under s 5 of the Defamation Act 1952:

> "In an action for defamation in respect of words containing two or more distinct charges against the pursuer a defence of justification shall not fail by reason only that the truth of every charge is not proved if the words not proved to be true do not materially injure the pursuer's reputation having regard to the truth of the remaining charges."

Under s 8 of the Rehabilitation of Offenders Act 1974 a pursuer who proves that the defender has maliciously published details of a spent conviction may recover damages.

### Innocent dissemination

Under s 1 of the Defamation Act 1996 it is a defence if the defender can show that he was not the author, editor or publisher of the matter which was complained of, and that he took reasonable care in relation to its publication and that he did not know or have reason to believe that what he did caused or contributed to the publication of the defamatory matter.

## Offer of amends

Sections 2–4 of the Defamation Act 1996 make provision for offer of amends in relation to defendants who did not know, or had no reason to believe, that the statement in question referred to the claimant and was untrue and defamatory of him.

## Absolute privilege

There are certain occasions in which it is for the benefit of the public that a person should be able to speak or write freely. Such a right over-rides the right not to be defamed.

### Parliamentary proceedings

Statements which are made in either House and reports in *Hansard* are completely protected: Parliamentary Papers Act 1840. Provisions which are contained in an Act of the Scottish Parliament are also protected: s 17 of the Defamation Act 1996, as amended by the Scotland Act 1998. Statements which are made in proceedings of the Scottish Parliament and any publication of any statement which is authorised by the Scottish Parliament are also absolutely privileged: s 41 of the Scotland Act 1998.

### Judicial proceedings

Absolute privilege attaches to all statements which are made in judicial proceedings: *Hebditch v MacIllwaine* (1894). However, protection does not extend to entirely irrelevant answers to a question put to a witness. In Scotland there is no absolute privilege in relation to civil proceedings: *Neill v Henderson* (1901). Fair and accurate reports of judicial proceedings are also absolutely privileged: s 14 of the Defamation Act 1996 (as amended).

### Executive matters

Communications between certain officers of state are privileged. However, it is difficult to say how high up the hierarchy the maker of the statement must be in order to be covered by absolute privilege. In *Chatterton v Secretary of State for India* (1895) a letter from the Secretary of State for India to his Parliamentary Under-Secretary was covered by absolute privilege.

## Qualified privilege

There are circumstances in which, on grounds of public policy and convenience, the law should allow the defender to make defamatory statements of the pursuer. However, such circumstances are less compelling than those in relation to which absolute privilege applies. In contrast to defamatory statements to which absolute privilege attaches, the defence of qualified privilege is vitiated by malice.

The categories of occasions which are covered by the defence of qualified privilege are not closed. It should also be stressed that there is some overlap between categories "(a)" and "(b)" and they should not, therefore, be regarded as hermetically sealed.

### (a) Where A has a legal, moral or social duty to communicate a statement to B, and B has a corresponding interest in receiving the statement, or, where A has an interest to be protected, and B is under a corresponding legal, moral or social duty to protect that interest

In *Stuart* v *Bell* (1891) it was held that the question of moral or social duty to communicate the relevant statement was a matter for the judge. According to Lindley LJ, "moral or social duty" meant a duty which was recognised by English people of ordinary intelligence and moral principle, but at the same time, not a duty which is enforceable by legal proceedings, whether civil or criminal.

In the majority of cases, the interest which is being protected is either a property, a business or a financial interest. However, other forms of interest have been recognised. For example, it has been held that a complaint to a bishop that a clergyman in the former's diocese had got into a fight with a schoolmaster was covered by qualified privilege: *James* v *Boston* (1846). Again, in *Seray Wurie* v *Charity Commission of England and Wales* (2009) it was held that the publication of a report of inquiry held by the Charity Commission attracted qualified privilege.

In *Fraser* v *Mirza* (1993) a complaint to the Chief Constable, which was made about a police constable by a member of the public, was held to be covered by qualified privilege. However, if the defender complains to the wrong person, he loses the defence of qualified privilege: *Beach* v *Freeson* (1972). A person who gives a job reference is covered by qualified privilege: *Farquhar* v *Neish* (1890). However, if a defamatory reference is also negligently made, it may attract liability in the law of negligence: *Spring* v *Guardian Assurance* (1995).

Statements which are made to the public at large will, generally speaking, not attract the defence of qualified privilege. However, a newspaper may be covered by qualified privilege in relation to the defamatory contents of an article which is published to the world at large: *Reynolds v Times Newspapers Ltd* (2001). In order for the defence to apply, so-called "responsible journalism" is required of the defender. The checklist (which is not exhaustive) as to whether an article is privileged in such circumstances depends upon a number of factors which include the seriousness of the allegation made; the nature of the allegation; the nature of the information; the source of the information; whether steps were taken to verify the information; and whether comment was sought from the pursuer.

The application of the *Reynolds* defence is seen in *GKR Karate v Yorkshire Post Newspapers Ltd (No 2)*. In that case, an article which appeared in a local newspaper which circulated in the Leeds area, made allegations about the claimant's conduct in selling karate lessons. It was alleged that the standard of lessons which were offered, was of an inferior nature. The article warned members of the public not to buy lessons from the claimant's door-to-door salesmen. It was held, at first instance, that the defendant newspaper could avail itself of the defence of qualified privilege, on the grounds that the public in Leeds had a legitimate interest in receiving the information, and the defendant newspaper was under a social and moral duty to communicate to the public in Leeds the particular information which was contained in the article. It was also in the public interest that the defendant published the information which was the subject matter of the action. See also *Grobbelaar v News Group Newspapers Ltd* (2001) where the claimant was a well-known football player. The *Sun* newspaper published a series of articles which alleged that he had taken bribes to fix football matches. The various publications complained of consisted of a series of vitriolic accusations. The language used was emotive and the articles had been calculated to embarrass not only the claimant, but also his wife and children. It was held by the Court of Appeal that the defence of qualified privilege did not apply.

The *Reynolds* defence was discussed again in the House of Lords case of *Jameel v Wall Street Journal Europe SPRL* (2006). For Lord Bingham (at 28) *Reynolds* built on the traditional foundations of qualified privilege but carried the law forward in a way which gave much greater weight than formerly to the value of informed public debate of significant public issues. In turn, for Lord Hoffman (at 46) the word "privilege" which was used in *Reynolds* was clearly not used in the old sense. It was the material which was privileged, not the occasion on which it was published. The *Reynolds* defence was a different jurisprudential creature from the traditional form of privilege from which it sprang. It might more appropriately be called the *Reynolds* public interest defence.

The so-called *Reynolds* defence was discussed again in the Supreme Court in *Flood v Times Newspapers Ltd* (2012). In that case, the claimant, who was a serving police officer, brought an action in defamation against the defendant in relation to the content of an article which had been published by the defendant. The article was published both in conventional newspaper form and also on the defendant's website. The article included information which had originally been contained in a press statement which had been issued by the police. The article also named the claimant, who had not been named, in the police press statement. A police investigation was instigated against the claimant. However, no evidence was found to support the allegations which had been made against him. He then returned to his post. After the conclusions of the investigation were communicated to the defendant, the original article remained un-amended on its website. The claimant sued the newspaper. The defendant relied on the defence of qualified privilege. The trial judge held that both the newspaper hard copy and the website versions of the article, attracted qualified privilege by way of the *Reynolds* defence, up to the date the defendant learned of the conclusions of the police investigation. After that date, the defence no longer applied. The Court of Appeal held that by virtue of the defendant having failed to take sufficient steps to verify the details of the allegations against the claimant, the defendant's publication did not constitute responsible journalism and, therefore, did not attract qualified privilege. The defendant successfully appealed to the Supreme Court. The sole question which the Supreme Court was required to answer was whether the publication of the article attracted the *Reynolds* defence. The Supreme Court held that qualified privilege existed where the public interest justified publication, notwithstanding that it carried the risk of defaming an individual who would have no remedy. In order to determine whether such privilege arose, a balance had to be struck between the desirability that the public should receive the information, and the potential harm which might be caused if the individual were defamed. The overriding test was that of responsible journalism. In essence, the *Reynolds* defence ranked as a "public interest" defence. In order to ascertain whether the defence was applicable, the starting point was to consider whether the subject-matter of the article was of public interest. Privilege arises not simply because of the circumstances of publication but because of the subject-matter of the publication itself. Importantly, the court considers both the subject-matter and the content of the article and also the appropriateness of publishing it. It is for the court to determine whether any publication is in the public interest.

We have seen above in the case of *Wright and Greig* (1890) that the person who circulates a slander is equally liable with the person who defamed the pursuer in the first place. An interesting point here in the context of the *Reynolds* defence is whether a journalist who simply repeats in an article which he has written a defamatory statement which has been made by someone else, can avail himself of the defence of qualified privilege. *"Reportage"* was described by Simon Brown LJ in *Al-Fagih v HH Saudi Research and Marketing (UK) Ltd* (2002) as a convenient word to describe the neutral reporting of attributed allegations, rather than their adoption by the newspaper. The issue of *reportage* as well as the *Reynolds* defence arose again in the Court of Appeal case of *Roberts v Gable* (2007). In that case, the claimants were two brothers who were both active members of the British National Party (BNP). The claimants complained of an article which had been published in a magazine called *Searchlight*. The offending article referred to a feud between different factions in the BNP in the London area, and referred to defamatory allegations (that, *inter alia*, the first claimant had stolen money collected at a BNP rally and both claimants had threatened to torture and kneecap certain individuals) which had previously been made in another publication entitled *British Nationalist*. The defendants, the publishers of *Searchlight,* claimed that the activities of prominent members of a political party were always matters of public interest, therefore the *Reynolds* defence applied, and, furthermore, that the defendants were merely reporting allegations without either adopting or endorsing them. In other words, the offending words which were published in *Searchlight* were pure *reportage*. The court held that the repetition rule and *reportage* were not in conflict with each other. The former rule was concerned with justification (or *veritas*) and the latter was concerned with privilege. A true case of *reportage* could provide a journalist with a complete defence of qualified privilege. If the journalist does not establish the defence of qualified privilege, the repetition rule is brought into play and the journalist has to prove the truth of the defamatory words. To qualify as *reportage*, the report must have the effect of reporting not the truth of the statements but the fact that they were made. There was no need for the journalist to take steps to verify the accuracy of the allegations. The protection which is accorded by the defence of *reportage* will be lost if the journalist adopts the report and makes it his own, or if he fails to report the story in a fair, disinterested and neutral way. The court went on to hold that the requirements which were listed as necessary for the special nature of *reportage* had still to be met. The court held that to satisfy the test of responsible journalism as adjusted to accommodate *reportage* there was no reason to confine the defence to "scandal-mongering". It could apply to serious allegations. The critical question was whether the public had the right to know that the relevant accusations were being made. Furthermore, in order for the defence of *reportage* to apply, there was no need for the claimant to be a public figure.

### (b) Protection of a common interest

One can also avail oneself of the defence of qualified privilege if one communicates a defamatory statement in protection of an interest which is shared with the person with whom one communicates. In *Watt v Longsdon* (1930) B was a foreign manager of X Co. B wrote to Y, a director of X Co, a letter which contained gross charges of immorality, drunkenness and dishonesty on the part of the claimant who was managing director of the company abroad. B also wrote a letter to the claimant's wife along similar lines. The Court of Appeal held that the letter to Y was covered by qualified privilege, but not the letter to the claimant's wife.

### (c) Statutory privilege

The common law has accorded qualified privilege to material such as accurate reports of judicial proceedings: *MacLeod v Justices of the Peace of Lewis* (1892). However, the importance of common law qualified privilege has been reduced by the advent of statutory qualified privilege, for example that under Sch 1 to the Defamation Act 1996.

### Loss of privilege

Privilege will be lost if (a) it is exceeded or (b) the defender is prompted by malice.

### (a) Excess of privilege

Statements which are quite unconnected with the main statement which is capable of attracting qualified privilege would deprive the defendant of the defence of qualified privilege. For example, in *Tuson v Evans* (1840) the defendant made a claim against the claimant for rent arrears. The defendant added: "This attempt to defraud me of the produce of land is as mean as it is dishonest." This wholly unnecessary addition deprived the defender of the defence of qualified privilege.

Privilege will also be lost if the defamatory matter is published to more persons than necessary: *De Buse* v *McCarthy* (1942).

## (b) Malice

If the defamatory publication is motivated by spite, or it is used for some improper motive, the defence will be lost: *Grobbelaar* (2001).

The court will be prepared to hold that the defender is motivated by malice if he does not believe in the truth of his statement, or was reckless as to whether the statement was true or false, or if he told a blatant lie: *Fraser* v *Mirza* (1993). Honest belief in the veracity of one's statement will allow the defence to succeed: *Horrocks* v *Lowe* (1975). However, even if the defender thinks his statement is true, the defence of qualified privilege will be lost if the defender's main intention is to harm the pursuer. If the defender's motives are mixed, the improper motive must be the dominant one in order for the defence to be lost.

## Fair comment

The defence of fair comment was reviewed by the Supreme Court in *Joseph* v *Spiller* (2010) which is the leading case on the subject. The facts of the case were simple. The claimants were members of a group of musicians. In 2004, one of the claimants, who was the manager of the group, agreed that the group's live acts could be promoted by the defendants, which was an advertising agency. The terms and conditions of the agreement included a re-engagement clause which provided that any further bookings should be arranged through the defendants. In 2007, the defendants complained to the claimants that the latter had arranged a performance directly with a venue, in breach of that condition. The claimants replied to the defendants by e-mail. The reply stated: "your contract ... holds no water in legal terms". The defendants responded quickly to that e-mail. The defendants posted a notice on their website. That notice announced that the defendants were no longer accepting bookings for the claimants as, "following a breach of contract [the first claimant] had advised that the terms and conditions of ... contracts hold no water in legal terms". The claimants brought libel proceedings against the defendants, averring that the statement which had been posted on their website, meant that the claimants were grossly unprofessional and also that they were untrustworthy. The defendants claimed, *inter alia*, the defence of fair comment. The Supreme Court decided in favour of the defendants. The court set out the following requirements for the defence of fair comment to succeed:

(a) the relevant statement must be comment, not fact;

(b) the matter in respect of which the comment is made is in the public interest;

(c) where that matter consists of facts which are alleged to have occurred, the facts are true;

(d) the comment is fair; and

(e) the statement is not made maliciously.

We will now look at each requirement in turn.

### (a) The relevant statement must be comment as opposed to fact

The defence of fair comment applies only if the words which are complained of are comment as opposed to fact. In short, the words must be an expression of opinion. For example, if a journalist were to state of X, a Member of Parliament in his newspaper article "X is a disgrace to his constituency", this would be a statement of fact. However, if the journalist had written "X has not attended Parliament for months, therefore, *X is a disgrace to his constituency*", the italicised phrase would rank as a comment.

The test which the courts employ to distinguish fact from comment is objective: *London Artists Ltd* v *Littler Grade Organisation Ltd* (1969). The intention of the maker of the statement is quite irrelevant in relation to how the courts interpret the words. However, it is sometimes difficult to ascertain whether certain words are, indeed, opinion or fact. For example, in *Dakhyl* v *Labouchere* (1908) the plaintiff was described as, "a quack of the rankest species". The House of Lords held that this could be comment.

### (b) The matter in respect of which the comment is made is in the public interest

The subject in respect of which the comment is made must be in the public interest. In the Court of Appeal case of *London Artists Ltd* v *Littler* (1969) Lord Denning MR was of the opinion that what ranked as public interest was not to be confined within narrow limits. His Lordship went on to state that whenever a matter is such as to affect people at large, so that they may be legitimately interested in, or concerned at, what is going on, or what might happen to themselves or others, then it is a matter of public interest on which everyone is entitled to make fair comment. Several examples can be given as to what the courts consider to be in the public interest. The closure of a theatrical play (*London Artists* v *Littler Grade Organisation Ltd* (1969)); the conduct of those in public office (*Campbell* v *Spotiswood* (1863)) and also the conduct of a publishing house (*Kemsley* v *Foot* (1951)) have been deemed to fall within the public interest.

### (c) Where the matter consists of facts which are alleged to have occurred, the facts are true

In order to attract the defence of fair comment, the relevant comment must be based on true facts, or statements which are privileged; for example, statements which are made in court by a witness: *London Artists* v *Littler Grade Organisation Ltd* (1969). In other words, the defender cannot fabricate facts, and then comment on those non-existent facts. Not all the facts require to be stated in the comment. However, in such a case the comment requires to be based on a sufficient substratum of fact: *Kemsley* v *Foot* (1952). The comment should also identify the subject-matter on which it is based in order to enable the reader to form his own view of the validity of the comment: *Joseph* v *Spiller* (2010). In *Joseph* it was emphasised that the rationale for the creation of the defence of fair comment was the desirability that a person should be entitled to express his views freely about a matter of public interest. If the subject-matter of the comment was not apparent from the comment, this justification for the defence would be lacking. The defamatory comment would be wholly unfocused. However, where the adverse comment is made generically, or generally, on matters which are in the public domain, there is no requirement that it is a prerequisite for the defence of fair comment to succeed, that the readers should be in a position to evaluate the comment for themselves. An example of this could be a newspaper article on the performance of a well-known football team. However, it may be difficult to decide what falls within the public domain and therefore, one can assume that the reader will automatically be familiar with the relevant facts in relation to which the comments are made. For example, in *Telnikoff* v *Matusevitch* (1992) the defendant wrote an letter which was published in the *Daily Telegraph* which was highly critical of an article which had been published in a previous edition of the same newspaper. The House of Lords held that the question as to whether the words which were complained of were capable of constituting statements of fact (that is, in order to determine whether the defence of fair comment could be sustained) was to be determined by consideration of the contents of the letter alone.

Sometimes the pursuer is not able to prove the truth of all the facts on which he has made adverse comment. Section 6 of the Defamation Act 1952 provides that in an action for defamation, the defence of fair comment shall not fail, "by reason only that the truth of every allegation of fact is not proved if the expression of opinion is fair comment having regard to such of the facts alleged to in the words complained of as are proved".

### (d) The comment is fair

An objective test is used by the court to ascertain whether the comment in question is fair (*Merrivale* v *Carson* (1887)). Wide latitude is given to the defender by the courts as to whether the comment is fair.

### (e) The statement

The defence of fair comment is vitiated if the defender is motivated by spite. In *Joseph* v *Spiller* (2010) the Supreme Court expressed the view that in ascertaining whether the defender is so motivated, one should adopt an objective approach and ask the question, "could an obstinate and prejudiced person honestly have based the comment which was made by the defendant on the facts on which the defendant commented?"

### Fair retort

A person against whom an allegation has been made publicly is permitted to deny that charge in strong language. Judicial indulgence is given to the defender here. However, he has no *carte blanche* to defame the pursuer. For example, in *Milne* v *Walker* (1893) the pursuer wrote a letter to a newspaper in which he claimed that the defender had supplied him with inferior goods. The defender replied in such terms as to insinuate that the pursuer was a liar. It was held that the defence of fair retort was inapplicable, on the basis that the defender had simply accused the pursuer of lying and could, therefore, not avail himself of the defence of fair retort.

The leading case on the defence of fair retort is now the Inner House case of *Curran* v *Scottish Daily Record and Sunday Mail Ltd* (2012). In that case, a Member of the Scottish Parliament sought damages from a newspaper company in relation to alleged defamatory statements which were contained in a newspaper article. The article was based on an interview with an MSP (Tommy Sheridan) who had previously belonged to the same party as the pursuer. In that article, Sheridan had branded the pursuer a "scab". The article also contained a photograph of the pursuer, with the word "scab" superimposed on it. Sheridan's comments followed in the wake of his success in a defamation action, and also following the publication of a statement by the pursuer and others to the effect that Sheridan had lied during the case. The pursuer had also been quoted in a newspaper calling the MSP a liar. The court held that Sheridan was entitled to give a robust response to being called a liar. Sheridan's riposte to the allegations which had been made against him by the pursuer should not be weighed on too fine a scale. In the last analysis, his response came within the parameters of fair retort.

### *Rixa*

This defence is concerned with words which are spoken in anger. In short, the courts show some indulgence to words which are so spoken. However, there is no defence if a definite or distinct charge of crime or dishonesty is made against the pursuer: *Christie* v *Robertson* (1899).

## VERBAL INJURY

The term "verbal injury" has been used since towards the end of the 19th century and has become associated with words which were not defamatory but which nevertheless harmed the pursuer: *Paterson* v *Welch* (1902). See also *Steele* v *Scottish Daily Record* (1970). In order to succeed under this head it must be shown that:

(1) the words are false;
(2) the defender intends to injure the pursuer; and
(3) the pursuer is injured.

Verbal injury includes slander of title, property and business. There is no liability if the words complained of are in defence of one's own property.

## CONVICIUM

Words which are published maliciously, and are calculated to bring the pursuer into public hatred or contempt have been categorised as a separate head of action. However, in the author's view, this is probably not a separate head of action in Scots law: *Steele* v *Scottish Daily Record* (1970). Rather, it is simply one way of being harmed by words. *Convicium* is a form of verbal injury, it is suggested. There is little modern authority on *convicium* in Scots law.

---

### Essential Facts

- There is no need for a defamatory statement to be published to a third party for liability to lie in Scots law.
- A defamatory statement is one which tends to lower the reputation of the pursuer in the minds of others.
- It is a question of law whether the words in question are defamatory.
- The courts adopt an objective approach in ascertaining the meaning of words.
- Words which are innocent in themselves may bear some secondary defamatory meaning. This is called an innuendo.
- The defamatory statement need not be in words.
- The person who is defamed must be living. One's reputation dies with one.
- A juristic person, such as a bank, can sue under the law of defamation provided that its professional reputation is struck at.
- The words which are complained of must refer to the pursuer.
- The pursuer must aver, but need not prove, that the statement is false.
- It is a complete defence to publish something which is true.
- There are certain occasions where a defamatory statement is covered by the defence of absolute privilege. Malice on the part of the defender is irrelevant.
- There are certain occasions when a defamatory statement is covered by the defence of qualified privilege. Malice on the part of the defender vitiates the defence.
- It is a defence if the defamatory statement is fair comment on a matter of public interest.

## Essential Cases

**Sim v Stretch (1936)**: definition of "defamatory".

**Lewis v Daily Telegraph (1964)**: the court decides how the ordinary man or woman would analyse the article in question.

**Tolley v Fry (1931)**: an advert is capable of bearing an innuendo.

**Hulton v Jones (1910)**: irrelevant at common law that the defendant did not wish to refer to the plaintiff.

**Reynolds v Times Newspapers (2001)**: defence of qualified privilege and articles in newspapers etc. Significance of "responsible journalism".

**Joseph v Spiller (2010)**: regarding the defence of fair comment, the court decided that the statement must be comment not fact, the matter in respect of which comment made is in the public interest; and alleged relevant facts to be true, comment to be fair and statement not to be made maliciously.

**Kemsley v Foot (1952)**: defence of fair comment and substratum of fact.

# 7 BREACH OF CONFIDENCE

In this chapter we look at liability in the law of delict in relation to the unauthorised use of information which relates to the pursuer. For example, if I were a famous person and I gave photographs of me which were taken on my holiday to my friend, David, to simply look at and he, nevertheless, sold them to a national newspaper which proceeded to publish the photographs, would the law of delict provide me with any redress against either David or the newspaper, or against both?

In *AG* v *Observer Ltd* (1990) (the *Spycatcher* case) Lord Keith of Kinkel stated that the law has long recognised that an obligation of confidence can arise out of a particular relationships such as that of doctor and patient, priest and penitent, solicitor and client and banker and customer. Furthermore, the obligation of confidence may be imposed by an express, or implied, term in a contract, but the obligation may also exist independently of any contract, on the basis of the equitable principle of confidence.

In *Pollard* v *Photographic Co* (1889) a photographer, who had taken a negative likeness of a lady to supply her with copies for money, was restrained by means of an injunction from selling or exhibiting copies, on the grounds that there was an implied contract not to use the negative for such purposes, but also that such a sale or exhibition was a breach of confidence. More recently, in *Duchess of Argyll* v *Duke of Argyll* (1967) the claimant sought to restrain the defendant, from whom she had been divorced, from communicating to a newspaper information of an intimate nature about her, and also to restrain the newspaper from publishing the information. The claimant succeeded in her action. The court held that a breach of confidence or trust can arise quite independently of any right of property or contract. Ungoed-Thomas J stated that there could hardly be anything more intimate or confidential than that which is involved in a matrimonial relationship or than in the mutual trust and confidences which are shared between husband and wife. Importantly, His Lordship went on to hold that an injunction could be granted to restrain the publication of confidential information not only by the person who was party to the confidence but also by others. Finally, His Lordship held that it was up to the court to decide whether the communications which were the subject-matter of the action were of such a confidential nature that they warranted protection under the law.

Several years later, liability for breach of confidence was considered in *Coco* v *A N Clark (Engineers) Ltd* (1969). In that case the manufacturer of a moped engine which was designed by Coco disclosed details of the workings of his engine to a number of potential manufacturers, including the defendant company, in order to ascertain the commercial viability of his product. However, the negotiations with the defendant company were unsuccessful. The defendant then allegedly made use of confidential information which was acquired during the discussion period in order to produce an engine which bore a similarity to Coco's engine. Coco sought an injunction in order to prevent the defendants from manufacturing their engine, on the basis that the defendants were using confidential information without the claimant's consent. Where as there was no formal contractual agreement between Coco and the defendants, Megarry J held the defendants liable. In His Lordship's view, for one to be liable for breach of confidence, first, the information itself must have the necessary quality of confidence about it; second, that information must have been disclosed in circumstances which give rise to an obligation of confidence; and, third, the information must be used in an unauthorised way, and so cause loss or detriment to the owner of the information.

More recently, the House of Lords had the opportunity to discuss the nature and extent of the concept of breach of confidence in *Campbell* v *Mirror Group Newspapers Ltd* (2004). In that case, the claimant, who was an internationally famous fashion model, volunteered information to the media about her private life. She claimed, untruthfully, that she did not take drugs. The defendant newspaper published articles which disclosed her drug addiction, and the fact that she was having therapy by means of a self-help group. The articles gave details of the group meetings she was attending and also showed photographs of her in a street as she was leaving a group meeting. She accepted that the newspaper was entitled to publish the fact of her drug addiction and the fact that she was receiving treatment, but claimed that the newspaper had acted in breach of confidence by obtaining and publishing details of her therapy and the photographs which had been taken of her covertly. The newspaper denied the claim, on the ground that it was entitled, in the public interest, to publish the information in order to correct the claimant's misleading statements. The newspaper also asserted that the information that it had published about her treatment was peripheral and was not sufficiently significant to amount to a breach of confidence. However, the House ruled in favour of the claimant. Lord Nicholls was of the view that the law imposes a duty of confidence whenever a person receives information which he either knows, or ought to know, is fairly and reasonably to be regarded as confidential. The essence of the tort was better encapsulated as misuse of private information. His Lordship went on to say that whereas formerly, the action of breach of confidence was founded on some prior confidential relationship, this was not the case in the modern law. The underlying question was whether the information which was disclosed was private and not public. There had to be some interest of a private nature which the claimant wished to protect. The question that one should ask was what a reasonable person of ordinary sensibilities would feel if she were placed in the same position as the claimant. The claimant's attendance at a drugs clinic was, indeed, sufficiently private to import a duty of confidence. For Baroness Hale, the important question was whether the defendant ought to know that there is a reasonable expectation that the information in question will be kept confidential.

The issue of tortious liability for breach of confidence came before the House of Lords again in *Douglas* v *Hello! Ltd (No 3)* (2008). The facts of that case were simple indeed. The first and second claimants were well-known film actors who had entered into an agreement with the third claimant, the publisher of an English celebrity magazine called *OK!* The Douglases granted *OK!* exclusive rights to publish photographs of their wedding. Wedding guests were informed that no photographs were to be taken. Also, tight security measures were put in place. However, despite those measures the wedding reception was infiltrated by a freelance photographer who surreptitiously took photographs. He then sold the exclusive right to publish the unauthorised photographs to the first defendant, *Hello!*, which was the publisher of a celebrity magazine which was in competition with the third claimant. The House of Lords held that whereas information about the wedding was information which anyone was free to communicate, the photographic images of the wedding were not publicly available and were, therefore, confidential information which warranted protection in law. A duty of confidence was owed *both* to the Douglases *and* to the publishers of *OK!* magazine.

For Lord Hoffmann, the fact that the information happened to have been about the personal life of the Douglases was irrelevant as far as the action for breach of confidence was concerned. The subject-matter of the action could have been anything which a newspaper was willing to pay for. What mattered was the fact that the Douglases, by the way in which they arranged their wedding, were in a position to impose an obligation of confidence. The Douglases were in control of the information which had commercial value.

The action for breach of confidence is not confined to media intrusion. Rather, it extends to the misuse of private information by private individuals. In *McKennitt* v *Ash* (2008) the claimant was a famous musician. She raised an action against the defendant who had written a book which contained intimate details of the personal relationship which the latter had had with the claimant. At first instance, an injunction was granted to prevent further publication of a significant part of the work which was complained of, on the ground that such information constituted private information, the misuse of which fell within the ambit of both the tort of breach of confidence and also Art 8 of the ECHR (which protects the right to respect for private and family life).

The law relating to misuse of private information was summarised in the Court of Appeal case of *Murray* v *Express Newspapers Ltd* (2009) (which was a striking-out action). The claimant (an infant) was the son of the famous author Joanne Murray (J K Rowling). One day, when the claimant and his parents were out walking in an Edinburgh street, the defendant took a colour photograph of the family group. The newspaper publisher settled the proceedings against it. On an application by the photographic agency, the judge struck out a claim against it on the basis that innocuous conduct in a public place or routine activities, such as a simple walk down the street or a visit to the shops, as distinct from engagement in family or sporting activities, did not attract any reasonable expectation of privacy. The claimant appealed successfully. The Court of Appeal held that the questions which fell to be answered in relation to a case where the subject-matter was the misuse of private information were, first, whether the information was private in the sense that it is, in principle, protected by Art 8 and, if so, second, whether, in all the circumstances, the interests of the owner of the information must yield to the right of freedom of expression conferred on the publisher by Art 10 (which protects freedom of expression but, at the same time, recognises the need to protect the rights and freedom of others).

In order to answer the first question, one had to ascertain whether the claimant had an expectation of privacy. That was an objective question. The approach which was taken by the House of Lords in *Campbell* was endorsed. The question as to whether there was a reasonable expectation of privacy was a broad one which took into account all the circumstances of the case. Such circumstances included the attributes of the claimant, the nature of the activity in which the claimant was engaged, the place at which it was happening, the nature of the intrusion, the absence of consent, whether such absence of consent was known or could be inferred, the effect on the claimant, and also the circumstances in which and the purposes for which the information came into the hands of the publisher. In the instant case, as to whether the claimant had a reasonable expectation of privacy, one was required to ask how a reasonable person in the position of the claimant would feel if the photograph were published. That was a question of fact.

As far as the second question was concerned, the court expressed the view that in balancing the respective rights which were conferred by Arts 8 and 10, it would (or might) be relevant to consider whether the claimant would consider the publication of the photograph highly offensive. It was, at least, arguable in the last analysis, that the claimant had a reasonable expectation of privacy. The issue of a child's right to privacy fell to be considered again by the Court of Appeal in *Weller* v *Associated Newspapers Ltd* (2015). In that case, photographs had been taken, by an unknown photographer, of children in a street while the children were out shopping with their father, a well-known musician. The defendant published an article in an online version of *The Mail*. The article contained photographs of the claimants and their father. The faces of the children had been pixelated. The claimants claimed damages for misuse of private information and/or breach of the Data Protection Act 1998. The court, in deciding in favour of the claimants, stated that whereas a child did not have a separate right of privacy, simply by virtue of being a child, there were several considerations relevant to children and not adults, which might mean that in a particular case, a child might have a reasonable expectation of privacy where an adult did not. See also *PJS* v *Newsgroup Newspapers Ltd* (2016).

We have now seen how the courts have generously expanded, with the aid of human rights jurisprudence, the "old" action for breach of confidence to embrace the protection of private information, in circumstances where the action is not based on a prior confidential relationship between the defender and the pursuer. However, how has human rights law impacted on the "old" action of breach of confidence, that is to say, in a situation where such an action is purely prefaced on a prior confidential relationship? This question fell to be addressed in the Court of Appeal case of *HRH Prince of Wales* v *Associated Newspapers Ltd* (2007). Here, the claimant, the Prince of Wales, kept handwritten travel journals in which he recorded his views and impressions of overseas visits. The journals were photocopied by a member of his private office and then circulated to chosen individuals in envelopes which were marked "private and confidential". Someone who was employed in the claimant's private office removed the journals from the claimant's office, and then supplied the defendant newspaper with copies of eight of the claimant's journals. The employee was employed under a contract which provided that any information she acquired during the course of her employment was subject to an undertaking of confidence, and was not to be disclosed to any unauthorised person. The defendant newspaper published substantial extracts from the journal which related to a visit by the Prince to Hong Kong in 1997 when the colony was handed over to the Republic of China. The claimant contended, *inter alia*, that such publication contravened his rights under Art 8 of the Convention, and also constituted a breach of confidence. The trial judge ruled in favour of the claimant. The defendant appealed.

As we can see here, the action stemmed from a breach of confidence which had been imposed on the person who had obtained the information in question. According to the Court of Appeal, the test which fell to be applied when considering whether it was necessary to restrict the freedom of expression of the newspaper in order to prevent disclosure of the relevant information which had originally been received in confidence, was whether in all the circumstances it was in the public interest that the duty of confidence should be breached. In the last analysis, the trial judge had been correct in deciding that the interference with Art 8 rights which had been "effected" by the newspaper's publication of information which was contained in the Prince's journal outweighed the significance of the interference with Art 10 rights which would have been involved had the newspaper been prevented from publishing that information.

## REMEDIES

Interdict is the primary remedy for a breach of confidence (Bell, *Commentaries*, vol 1, 111–12).

Damages can also be awarded where a breach of confidence has taken place (*Seager* v *Copydex (No 2)* (1969).

As an alternative to claiming damages for breach of confidence, it is possible that the pursuer may elect to require the defender to account for any profits which the person who has used the information has made from such use. There is little recent Scottish authority on this remedy.

## Essential Facts

- The obligation of confidence may arise out of a particular relationship, such as those of doctor and patient, solicitor and client and husband and wife.
- The essence of the delict of breach of confidence is the misuse of private information.
- There must be some interest of a private nature which the pursuer wishes to protect.
- In determining whether a confidence has been breached one should ask how a reasonable person of ordinary sensibilities would feel in relation to the transmission of the information if he were placed in the same position as the pursuer.
- The courts will impose a duty of confidence both on the person to whom the information has been confided within a particular relationship (such as husband and wife) and also on another person who subsequently acquires such information.
- If the relevant information is already in the public domain the court will not restrain its publication.
- If the publication of the information is in the public interest the court will not restrain its publication.

## Essential Cases

**AG v Observer Ltd (1990)**: the obligation of confidence may be imposed by an express or implied term in a contract, or by the independent equitable principle of confidence.

**Coco v A N Clark (Engineers) Ltd (1969)**: for one to be liable for breach of confidence, first, the information itself must have the necessary quality of confidence; second, that information must have been disclosed in circumstances which give rise to an obligation of confidence; and, third, the information must be used in an unauthorised way and so cause loss or detriment to the owner of the information.

**Campbell v MGN Ltd (2004)**: as far as the tort of breach of confidence is concerned, the underlying question is whether the information which is disclosed is private and not public. The question which one should ask is what a reasonable person of ordinary sensibilities would feel if placed in the same position as the claimant.

# 8 LIABILITY FOR ANIMALS

## THE OLD LAW

At common law the person who was in charge of an animal was strictly liable for any damage which was caused by the animal if:

(a) the animal was *ferae naturae* (that is, it belonged to a dangerous species); or

(b) the animal was *mansuetae naturae* (that is, it did not belong to a dangerous species but the animal had dangerous characteristics or tendencies).

Animals which fell within category "(a)" included lions, bears, wolves, apes and monkeys: see, for example, *Burton* v *Moorhead* (1880–81). Animals which fell within category "(b)" included bulls, horses and dogs.

As far as animals which fell into category "(a)" were concerned, the law imposed strict liability for injury which was caused by such animals. As far as "(b)" was concerned, liability lay if the animal concerned had evinced vicious tendencies in the past, and such tendencies were known, or should have been known to the animal's owner: *Renwick* v *Rotberg* (1875) and *Fraser* v *Bell* (1887). This would include the case where the animal concerned was potentially dangerous, only in a given situation. For example, in *McDonald* v *Smellie* (1903) a child was bitten by a dog which was not known to be generally vicious, but had in the past behaved dangerously to children. It was held that the defender was liable.

## THE MODERN LAW

The modern law which governs liability for harm which is caused by animals is now contained in the Animals (Scotland) Act 1987.

### Liability for injury and harm caused by an animal

Under s 1(1) of the 1987 Act, a person is liable for any injury or damage which is caused by an animal if:

(a) at the time of the injury or damage complained of he was the keeper of the animal;

(b) the animal belonged to a species whose members generally are by virtue of their physical attributes or habits likely (unless controlled or restrained) to injure severely or kill persons or animals, or damage property to a material extent; and

(c) the injury or damage complained of is directly referable to such physical attributes or habits.

For the purposes of s 1(1)(b), "species" includes sub-species: s 1(2). It is for the court to decide whether the requirements of s 1(1)(b) are satisfied: *Foskett* v *McClymont* (1998).

Under s 5, the keeper of an animal is defined as the owner of the animal, or the person who has possession of it, or the person who has the actual care and control of a child under the age of 16 who owns the animal or has possession of it.

Dogs, and dangerous wild animals within the meaning of s 7(4) of the Dangerous Wild Animals Act 1976 are deemed to be likely (unless controlled or restrained) to injure severely or kill persons or animals by biting or otherwise savaging, attacking or harrying. Also, cattle, horses and pigs *inter alia* are deemed to be likely to damage to a material extent land or the produce of land, whether harvested or not: s 1(3).

In *Fairlie* v *Carruthers* (1996) a large frisky and boisterous dog ran up to and knocked over an old lady who broke her leg as a consequence. The pursuer sued the keeper under the 1987 Act, but failed, on the basis that the dog had neither harried nor attacked her. Therefore, the injury which she suffered was not directly referable to the statutorily deemed propensities of the dog. Similarly, in *Welsh* v *Brady* (2009) a dog walker raised an action against another dog walker in respect of an injury which the former received when the latter's black Labrador collided with her while the dog was running at great speed. The pursuer founded her action both on s 1(1)(b) of the Animals (Scotland) Act 1987 and also in terms of the common law of negligence. In the Outer House the Lord Ordinary found against the pursuer in terms of both heads of action. She reclaimed. The Inner House was of the view that the form of injury which the pursuer had sustained was not attributable to the characteristics which fell within the scope of s 1(1)(b) of the Act. In essence, Labradors, by their very nature, are not likely to collide violently with individuals and injure them. The pursuer, therefore, failed in her action.

Under s 1(4), no liability lies in respect of any injury which is caused by an animal where the injury consists of disease which is transmitted by means which are unlikely to cause severe injury other than a disease. Therefore, if a monkey in a cage in a zoo coughs on a child and thereby infects him with an illness, the zoo would not be liable. However, liability would lie if the monkey were to escape from its cage and knock the child to the ground, the upshot of which the child receives cuts to his leg, and subsequently develops tetanus.

## The "old" law and the Act

The Act only replaces strict liability under the old law which pertained to dangerous animals: s 1(8). Liability in terms of the law of negligence remains for harm which is caused by animals: *Hill* v *Lovett* (1992); *Swan* v *Andrew Minto and Son* (1998) and *Wilson* v *Donaldson* (2004).

The Act also replaces liability in terms of injury which is caused by straying livestock in terms of the Winter Herding Act 1686 and damage which is inflicted to dogs and poultry in terms of the Dogs Act 1906.

## DEFENCES

### Contributory negligence

The Act excludes liability if the injury or damage was due wholly to the fault of the person sustaining it, or, in the case of an injury sustained by an animal, the fault of a keeper of the animal: s 2(1)(a).

### *Volenti*

The Act also excludes liability if the pursuer willingly accepted the risk of the injury which he sustained: s 2(1)(b).

### Specific defences

Under s 2(1)(c) it is a defence if the person or animal who sustained injury was as a result of the relevant person or animal coming on land which was occupied by a person who was a keeper, or by another person who authorised the presence on the land of the animal which caused the injury or damage; and, either:

(i) the person sustaining the injury or damage was not authorised or entitled to be on that land; or

(ii) no keeper of the animal sustaining the injury was authorised or entitled to have the animal present on that land.

As far as the defence under s 2(1)(c) is concerned, no defence lies if the animal which caused injury or damage was kept wholly or partly for the purpose of protecting persons or property unless the keeping of the animal on the premises and the use which was made of the animal was reasonable. If the animal was a guard dog within the meaning of the Guard Dogs Act 1975 no defence lies unless there was compliance with s 1 of that Act: s 2(2).

---

### Essential Facts

- Animals (Scotland) Act 1987 replaced the common law rules governing strict liability for injury caused by dangerous animals. Liability in terms of the law of negligence remains.

- Liability lies if the animal belongs to a species whose members generally are by virtue of their physical nature (unless controlled or restrained) to injure severely or kill persons or animals or damage property to a material extent.

- Certain defences apply including that of *volenti non fit iniuria* and contributory negligence.

# 9 BREACH OF STATUTORY DUTY

Acts of Parliament impose duties on both public authorities and private individuals. However, to what extent, if any, can an individual who has sustained harm because the person upon whom the duty is placed, has breached such a duty? While the action for breach of statutory duty might bear some superficial resemblance to the common-law action for negligence, which we have already discussed, the former action is quite separate and independent from the latter (*London Passenger Transport Board v Upson* (1949); *Chipchase* v *British Titan Products Co Ltd* (1956)).

## WHEN DOES AN ACTION FOR BREACH OF STATUTORY DUTY LIE?

A relatively small number of statutes specifically exclude an action for breach of statutory duty. For example, s 47(1) of the Health and Safety etc at Work Act 1974 excludes an action for breach of statutory duty in terms of a breach of ss 2–8 inclusive of that Act. Again, a few statutes expressly provide that a civil action can be brought in respect of a breach of a duty which the statute imposes. For example, s 73(6) of the Environmental Protection Act 1990 provides that a person who has suffered damage as a consequence of waste, which has been deposited in contravention of the Act, is made civilly liable for such a breach. However, in the vast majority of cases no such provision is made. The court must, therefore, ascertain whether the pursuer can sue for the defender's breach of the relevant statutory duty. In the last analysis, the court requires to ascertain the intention of Parliament. In determining whether the statute in question gives rise to an action for breach of statutory duty, the court is required to consider the whole statute and also the relevant circumstances, including the pre-existing law in which it was enacted: *Cutler* v *Wandsworth Stadium Ltd* (1949). This point was poignantly illustrated in the House of Lords case of *X v Bedfordshire CC* (1995). Essentially , the claimants claimed that social work and educational authorities had failed to exercise their respective statutory duties, the upshot of which was that the claimants (who were children at the time) had suffered harm. The claimants based their action, *inter alia,* on breach of statutory duty. The House held that there was no general rule for ascertaining whether a statute conferred a right on a private individual to sue for a breach of a statute. The breach of a statutory duty did not of itself confer a right to sue for such breach. However, such a right could arise if the relevant statute imposed a duty for the protection of a limited class of the public and there was a clear parliamentary intention to confer a private right of action on members of that class. In the instant case, the relevant statutes conferred no such private right of action.

## REQUIREMENTS TO SUCCEED IN AN ACTION FOR BREACH OF STATUTORY DUTY

We now look at the fundamental requirements which the pursuer requires to satisfy in order to succeed. The pursuer is required to prove that:

(1) the statute imposed a duty on the defender;
(2) the statute covers the circumstances of the case;
(3) the *raison d'être*, or purpose, of the statute was to protect the pursuer;
(4) Parliament, by means of the statute, intended to confer a private right of action on the pursuer;
(5) the defender has breached the statutory duty;
(6) the defender's breach of the statutory duty caused the harm in question;
(7) the pursuer has suffered harm of such a kind which the statute intended to prevent.

We will now look at each requirement in turn

### (1)  The statute imposes a duty on the defender

In order to succeed, the pursuer is required to prove that the statute in question imposed a duty (for example, a duty on an employer to fence dangerous machinery, or a duty on a public authority to provide adequate sewers, or provide educational facilities) on the defender, as opposed to a power. Importantly, the statutory duty must impose a duty on the defender himself: *ICC Ltd* v *Shatwell* (1965).

### (2)  The statute covers the circumstances of the case

The statutory duty must also relate to the very circumstances out of which the action springs. For example, in *Chipchase* v *British Titan Products Co Ltd* (1956) a workman was injured when he fell from a platform which was situated 6 feet above the ground. Statutory regulations provided that any working platform, from which a person was liable to fall more than 6 feet 6 inches, was required to be at least 34 inches wide. The claimant's action failed since the "evil" at which the statute in question sought to strike had no relevance to the facts of the case. See also *Kennedy* v *Cordia (Services ) LLP* (2016) and *Coia* v *Portavadie Estates Ltd* (2015).

## (3) The purpose of the statute was to protect the pursuer

The pursuer is required to prove that Parliament, by means of the relevant statute, intended to confer a benefit on the pursuer. The leading case on this point is *Cutler* v *Wandsworth Stadium Ltd* (1949). In that case, the claimant was a bookmaker. He raised an action against the defendant, a licensed dog track, which had refused to grant him space on the defendant's premises, to allow the claimant to carry on bookmaking. The claimant claimed that he had been denied access to the premises simply to safeguard the interests of the defendant, who operated its own bookmaking business (a totalisator). The claimant based his claim on s 11(2) of the Betting and Lotteries Act 1934 which provided that the track operator "shall take such steps as are necessary to secure that ... there is available for the bookmakers space on the track where they can conveniently carry on bookmaking in connection with dog races run on the track". However, the House of Lords held that the section was intended to ensure fair competition between bookmakers and the totalisator, and thereby protect the *public,* rather than protect bookmakers as a class. The claimant, therefore, failed in his action.

Again, in the House of Lords case of *Lonrho* v *Shell Petroleum (No 2)* (1982) Shell contracted to use Lonrho's pipeline in order to transport oil to Southern Rhodesia. In the same year as the contract was concluded, Southern Rhodesia declared unilateral independence, after which it was made a statutory offence to supply oil to that country, whereupon Shell ceased to use Lonrho's pipeline. However, Shell employed alternative means to supply Southern Rhodesia with oil, in contravention of the relevant legislation. Lonrho sued Shell for the loss which the former had sustained by Shell flouting the legislation. The House held that the relevant legislation was not intended to protect the interest of oil suppliers. Rather, the very purpose of the legislation was generally to undermine the illegal regime in Southern Rhodesia. Therefore, in the last analysis, the relevant statutes did not confer any benefit on the class of which Lonrho was a member. Lonrho, therefore, failed in its action against Shell.

## (4) Parliament intended to create a private right of action

While the pursuer requires to prove that the purpose of the relevant statute which has been breached was intended to protect him, the pursuer must go further and prove that the statute conferred on him a civil right to sue for such breach. In the last analysis, the court is required to consider the purpose of the whole Act: *Cutler* v *Wandsworth Stadium* (1949); *X* v *Bedfordshire CC* (1995). However, in order to ascertain whether the statute in question does confer a civil right of action, the courts have, over the years, formulated certain presumptions in order to assist them in this task. We now consider each presumption in turn.

### (a) The availability of alternative remedies

The first presumption is that where Parliament provides for an alternative remedy for the breach of statutory duty in question, the availability of such a remedy precludes a private right of action, by way of breach of statutory duty. For example, in *Atkinson* v *Newcastle and Gateshead Waterworks Co* (1847) the defendant company was placed under a duty by the Waterworks Clauses Act 1847 to fix fireplugs at intervals along the street and, furthermore, to keep the fireplugs charged up with water to the prescribed pressure. A fire broke out at the claimant's premises. However, there was insufficient water in the pipes to allow the fire to be fought satisfactorily. The claimant's premises were destroyed as a consequence. The claimant raised an action for breach of statutory duty against the defendant water company. However, the claimant failed in his action since the court held that the Act provided for the imposition of a fine in the face of its breach.

A modern case which emphasises the importance of the availability of alternative remedies is the House of Lords case of *Phelps v Hillingdon LBC* (2000). In that case, the defendant educational authority had failed to diagnose the plaintiff's dyslexia. She raised on action, *inter alia,* for breach of statutory duty against the defendant. However, in rejecting the claimant's appeal, the House held that the relevant legislation, which conferred both duties and powers on the defendant authority contained appeal procedures by means of which actions of the authority could be challenged. The claimant could also have invoked judicial review to secure redress.

However, simply because the relevant statute makes provision for an alternative remedy (for example, by way of a fine) in terms of the relevant statutory breach, an action for such breach may still lie, provided that the statute was intended to protect a particular class of individual. A good example of this principle is provided by the courts' approach to the application of the Factories Acts 1937 (repealed) and 1961 in terms of delictual liability for breach of statutory duty. The oft-cited example of such an approach is seen in *Groves v Lord Wimborne* (1898). In that case, the occupier of a factory was statutorily required to fence dangerous machinery. Contravention of the statute carried a fine of £100. The statute also provided that either the whole or part of the fine might, if the Secretary of State so determined, be payable to the injured employee. A boy, who was employed in the factory, caught his arm in part of a machine in the factory. The boy's arm required to be amputated. He sued his employer, founding his action on breach of statutory duty. The claimant succeeded. However, it requires to be added that, in deciding in favour of the claimant, the Court of Appeal emphasised that there was no guarantee that the victim would receive any part of the fine and, in any event, the statutory upper limit of £100 seemed, in the view of the court, insufficient compensation for death or very serious injury.

Furthermore, the courts are prepared to allow an action for breach of statutory duty if the relevant statute which has been breached contains no machinery for its enforcement, since, otherwise, the statute would be "toothless". For example, in *Dawson v Bingley DCC* (1911) in contravention of s 66 of the Public Health Act 1875 (repealed) the defendant provided a notice which indicated the wrong position of a fireplug in a street. A fire broke out at the plaintiff's premises. The fire brigade arrived promptly at the scene of the fire, but the brigade's rescue attempts were delayed, as a consequence of the statutory breach. The Court of Appeal held that, given the fact that the relevant statute made no provision for the enforcement of s 66, an action for breach of statutory duty would lie.

More recently, in *X (Minors) v Bedfordshire CC* (1995) Lord Browne-Wilkinson stated that "if the statute provides no other remedy for its breach and the Parliamentary intention to protect a limited class is shown, that indicates that there may be a private right of action". That is to say, that an action for breach of statutory duty could lie.

### (b) Does the common law provide an adequate remedy?

Conversely, if adequate commow-law remedies are available to the pursuer in the face of such a breach, a presumption against the imposition of an action by way of breach of statutory duty is raised. For example, in *J Bollinger v Costa Brava Wine Co Ltd* (1960) the defendants marketed a Spanish wine. They called their wine "champagne". The claimants manufactured champagne from the Champagne region of France. The claimants raised an action against the defendants, alleging infringement of the Merchandise Marks Act 1887. At first instance, the court held that the statute did not give the claimants a right to sue for breach of statutory duty. In reaching this decision the court was influenced by the fact that the Act specifically preserved the right of rival traders, such as the claimants, to raise an action against the defendant for passing off.

We have already seen in *Phelps*, above, that one of the reasons why the claimant failed in his action for breach of statutory duty was that one of the alternative remedies which was available to him was an action by way of judicial review. Therefore, the alternative remedy which raises a presumption against the imposition of statutory liability does not necessarily require to be a delictual remedy.

### (c) Was the type of harm which the pursuer sustained recognised by the common law?

If the harm which the pursuer sustained would not usually form the basis of an action at common law, a presumption is raised to the effect that an action for breach of statutory duty will not be available. For example, in the House of Lords case of *Pickering* v *Liverpool Daily Post and Echo Newspapers plc* (1991) the claimant claimed damages by way of an action for breach of statutory duty, relating to the publication of information about an application to a Mental Health Review Tribunal. The House, in rejecting the claimant's claim, held that whereas the publication of such information might not be in the claimant's interest, such a form of damage was not one which the common law recognised. Therefore, the claimant failed in his action.

However, on occasions, the courts have allowed an action for breach of statutory duty where the harm which the pursuer sustained has sounded in terms of pure economic loss in respect of which, as we have already seen (pp 22–23), the courts are not prepared to allow the pursuer to recover. For example, in *Monk* v *Warbey* (1935) the owner of a car, in contravention of s 35 of the Road Traffic Act 1935, permitted the car to be driven by an uninsured person (who was destitute of means) who collided with and injured the claimant. The claimant sued the car owner. One can see here that the loss in question simply ranked in nature as pure economic loss in that the defendant himself (as opposed to the driver of the car) had not physically injured the claimant. Rather, the defendant's conduct had placed the claimant in a position where his claim against the driver was worthless. However, the Court of Appeal held that the claimant could recover for breach of statutory duty.

## (d) Is the statutory duty specific in nature?

The more specific the duty which Parliament imposes on the defender, the more likely it is that the court will decide that an action for breach of statutory duty will lie. For example, the breach of a statute which places an employer under a duty to satisfactorily guard dangerous machinery, is more likely to form the basis of a successful action for breach of statutory duty than the breach of a statute which imposes general duties on social work or educational authorities: X *(Minors)* v *Bedfordshire CC* (1995).

## (e) Is the statute aimed at regulating public authorities?

If the relevant statute is intended to regulate, for example, the general administration of the prison service, there is a presumption that Parliament does not intend to confer a private right on the pursuer to sue in respect of any breach: R v *Deputy Governor of Pankhurt Prison, ex p Hague* (1992).

## (5) The defender breached the statutory duty

The pursuer is required to prove that the defender has breached the duty which statute has imposed on the latter. This has some overlap with sub-heading (2) on p 110.

To ascertain whether the statute has been breached simply involves one interpreting the relevant provision. Whereas some statutes, such as the Occupiers Liability (Scotland) Act 1960, s 2, imposes a duty to the effect that the potential defender take reasonable care, other statutes impose a higher standard, for example an absolute obligation on the defender. For example, in *Millar* v *Galashiels Gas Co Ltd* (1949) the pursuer's husband, M, was employed as a stoker in the defenders' gasworks. One day, M fell to the bottom of a liftshaft in the defender's gasworks. He was killed. The pursuer raised an action for breach of statutory duty against the defender. The Factories Act 1937, s 22(1) (repealed) required a hoist or lift to be of good mechanical construction, sound material and adequate strength, and be properly maintained. Section 152(1) (repealed) went on to define "maintained" as "maintained in an efficient state, in efficient working order and in good repair". The House of Lords held that the Act had imposed on the defender both an absolute, and also a continuing duty. In the last analysis, it was quite irrelevant that the defenders had not been negligent in maintaining the lift equipment.

It is common for health and safety legislation to require the relevant person, for example an employer to take measures which are "reasonably practicable" in the circumstances. Such a standard is less onerous than one which imposes absolute liability; see, eg, *Edwards* v *NCB* (1949) and *Neil* v *Greater Glasgow Health Board* (1996).

## (6) The breach of statutory breach caused harm to the pursuer

It must be proved that there was a causal link between the relevant statutory breach and the subsequent harm to the pursuer. This point can be neatly illustrated in the leading case of *McWilliam* v *Sir William Arrol and Co Ltd* (1962). Here, the pursuer's husband, M, fell from a steel lattice tower at a shipyard. M was killed. The defenders, in contravention of the relevant statute, had failed to provide M with a safety belt. However, it was proved that even if a safety belt had been provided, M would not have worn it. The House of Lords, therefore, held that since there was no causal link between the statutory breach and M's falling from the tower, the defenders were not liable.

## (7) The harm which the pursuer sustained was of a type which the statute intended to prevent

The pursuer is required to prove that the type of harm which he sustained was such that the relevant statute intended to prevent. This point is well illustrated in the leading case of *Gorris* v *Scott* (1874). In that case, the relevant statute provided that sheep and cattle were required to be carried in pens of certain specifications when being transported. The defendant flouted these provisions, the upshot of which was that the plaintiff's sheep were washed overboard and drowned, during rough weather. The accident would not have occurred if pens had been provided in accordance with the legislation. However, it was held that the intention of the statute was intended to prevent the spread of disease, as opposed to preventing sheep being washed overboard. The claimant, therefore, failed in his action.

## DEFENCES

The defences of contributory negligence, *volenti non fit injuria* and illegality apply to an action for breach of statutory duty (see Chapter 11).

## Essential Facts

- In certain circumstances, the court will allow the pursuer to recover damages if he has sustained harm as a result of breach of statutory duty.
- The action for breach of statutory duty is quite separate from an action in negligence.
- In deciding whether damages are recoverable for breach of statutory duty the court requires to ascertain the intention of Parliament.
- The pursuer requires to prove that: the statute imposed a duty on the defender; the statute covers the circumstances of the case; the purpose of the statute was to protect the pursuer; Parliament intended to confer a private action on the pursuer; the defender breached the statute; the defender's statutory breach caused the harm in question; and the pursuer has suffered harm which is of a kind which statute intended to prevent.

## Essential Cases

**Cutler v Wandsworth Stadium Ltd (1949)**: in determining whether the pursuer can recover for breach of statutory duty the court is required to consider the whole of the statute and also the relevant circumstances, including the pre-existing law, in which the statute was enacted.

**McWilliams v Sir William Arrol and Co Ltd (1962)**: there requires to be a causal link between the relevant statutory breach and the resultant harm to the pursuer.

**X v Bedfordshire CC (1995)**: the breach of a statutory duty does not of itself confer a right to sue for such breach. However, such a right could arise if the relevant statute imposed a duty for the protection of a limited class of the public and, also, that there was a clear Parliamentary intention to confer a private right of action on members of that class.

# 10 VICARIOUS LIABILITY

In this chapter we will look at the liability of employers for the actions of others. Accidents are often caused by those who are carrying out work for others. For example, an employee who performs his duties negligently, may injure a fellow worker or a member of the public. Sometimes, however, an accident occurs while someone who is not an employee of another person, is carrying out work for another person. For example, a taxi driver whom I have paid to take me to the railway station may negligently collide with a pedestrian on the way to the station. What has to be answered is whether the injured person can sue the person who is paying the person whose negligent conduct caused the accident in question. In short, subject to several limited exceptions, only an employer can be sued for the delicts which have been committed by his employee during the scope of his employment. One who simply pays someone to carry out work for him on an *ad hoc* basis cannot, normally, be sued if that person causes injury or damage. One cannot, therefore, normally be sued for a delict which is committed by an independent contractor. For example, in the example just given, I would not be liable to the person who was negligently knocked down by the taxi driver since, in the eye of the law, he would rank as an independent contractor.

It must be stressed at this juncture that an employer is liable for *all* delicts of his employee, not simply those based on the negligent conduct of the employee. For example, a proprietor of a newspaper could be sued for a defamatory article in its newspaper which has been written by a journalist of the newspaper. Also, in certain cases, as we shall see below, an employer can be sued for assaults which are perpetrated by employees who act as security staff.

Vicarious liability is of importance from a practical, as well as an academic viewpoint, in that, generally, pursuers are inclined to sue only those who are able to compensate them. For example, if I am negligently knocked over by an army private who is driving a military vehicle, it is preferable that I should sue the Crown which has much more money, of course, has much more money than the person who actually injured me. Similarly, if I am defamed in the column of a newspaper, it would be more prudent to sue the relevant newspaper proprietor rather than the journalist concerned.

It must be stressed that the law imposes vicarious liability on an employer simply by reason of his status, or relationship, with the person who inflicted the relevant harm. There is no requirement that the employer himself be negligent, in any way, for the relevant delict.

## EMPLOYER'S VICARIOUS LIABILITY IN DELICT

An employer is vicariously liable for the delicts of his *employee* if the delicts are committed within the scope of the latter's employment. However, the employer is not normally liable for the delictual conduct of an *independent contractor*. This concept was well ingrained in Scots law by the early 19th century: see, for example, *Baird* v *Hamilton* (1826).

### Employee or independent contractor?

We must, therefore, at the outset, ascertain whether the person who actually harmed the pursuer is either an employee or an independent contractor. An employee is employed under a contract of service, whereas an independent contractor is employed under a contract for services. Often it is easy to recognise a contract of service when one sees it. However, it is difficult to say wherein the distinction lies between a contract of service and a contract for services. A ship's master, a chauffeur, a reporter of a newspaper and a university lecturer are all employed under a contract of service, whereas a taxi driver and a newspaper contributor are employed under a contract for services.

A somewhat crude distinction between an employee and an independent contractor is that, whereas the former's work is integrated in the employer's business that of the latter is not. The "integration" test was first put forward by Denning LJ (as he then was) in *Stevenson, Jordan and Harrison Ltd* v *MacDonald* (1952). The test was applied in *Inglefield* v *Macey* (1967). In that case the claimant, who was self-employed, began to work with the defendant, a timberman. The arrangement between the two parties was that the claimant should retain his self-employed status. The defendant told the claimant what he wanted done and supplied the necessary equipment. The claimant did the work. The defendant did not, however, tell the claimant how to do the work, because the former knew the claimant had sufficient expertise. One day the claimant was injured while felling a tree. Ashworth J, adopting the "integration" test, held that the claimant was an independent contractor since his work, although done for the business, was accessory to it, and not integrated in it. While the "integration" test is superficially attractive, it may be difficult in practice to ascertain if the work of the individual in question is either integrated or, on the other hand, simply accessory to the business of the employer.

## Fact or law?

In *O'Kelly* v *Trusthouse Forte* (1984) the Court of Appeal held that whether the relevant relationship falls to be categorised either as one of service or one of services, is a question of law. However, it is up to the relevant court determining the issue, not only to ascertain the relevant facts, but also to assess them qualitatively. Only if the weight which is given by the court to a particular factor shows that the court has misdirected itself in law, can an appellate court interfere with the decision.

## Factors taken into account

In order to ascertain who is an employee and who is an independent contractor, the courts adopt a variety of tests. The most important are:

(1) To what extent, if any, does the person who pays the other have the right to *choose* who works for him? The right to choose is more consistent with a contract of service.

(2) *Payment of wages.* The fact that the individual is in receipt of regular payment from the employer is more consistent with a contract of service.

(3) To what extent, if any, can the person who is paying *control* the manner in which the tasks which the other has to perform are carried out? The greater the degree of control, the more likely it is that the relevant relationship is that of employer–employee. However, given that employees nowadays are carrying out much more technical and esoteric tasks than in the past, this test is losing some of its currency.

(4) The right of the employer to *hire and fire* the other is more consistent with a contract of service.

## FOR WHICH ACTS OF AN EMPLOYEE IS THE EMPLOYER LIABLE?

An employer is liable only for acts which are done in the course of the employee's employment. An employer will be liable for the conduct of his employees at the relevant place of employment during the hours for which the employee is employed, and also as long as the employee is on the premises concerned, within reasonable limits of time of the commencement and conclusion of the shift. In *Bell* v *Blackwood, Morton and Sons* (1960) the pursuer, a woman who was in the employment of a firm of carpet manufacturers, was jostled and knocked down by a fellow employee while descending a stair after the hooter had sounded for the end of the shift. The defenders were held vicariously liable for the conduct of the negligent employee.

## Frolics of employee

If an employee has gone on a frolic of his own, that is to say, he has failed to carry out his duties in the manner which his employer requires; such an act on the part of the employee will take him outside the course of his employment, and the employer is not liable for the acts of his employee.

### Deviation from authorised route

Sometimes the "frolic" comprises the employee going on a journey of his own, and being responsible for injuring someone in the course of that unauthorised journey. If the deviation by the employee from the normal or authorised journey is substantial, then the employer will not be liable. In *Storey* v *Ashton* (1869) a cart driver completed his employer's work and went to visit a relative. During the course of the journey, the carter injured the claimant. It was held that the employer was not liable for this tort, on the basis that the employee had gone on a frolic of his own. Again, in *Hilton* v *Burton* (1961) X, H and Y were building workers who were employed at a building site. H drove them to a café 7 miles away, in order to buy tea. X was killed by the negligent driving of H. It was held that H was not acting within the scope of his employment. Again, in *Williams* v *Hemphill* (1966) a bus driver, while carrying children, made a detour at the request of some of the children. The bus was involved in a collision. A passenger was injured. It was held that the driver was still acting within the scope of his employment, notwithstanding the fact that the deviation from the route which the bus driver's employers wished him to take was fairly substantial. See also *Smith* v *Stages* (1989).

### Other conduct

We now ask to what extent other forms of conduct (that is, apart from a situation where the employee has deviated from a given route) can take the employee outside the scope of his employment. It should be stressed that whilst the forms of wrongful conduct are discussed below under separate sub-headings, this is purely done for the sake of convenience. Often there is an overlap between each category.

## Effect of express prohibitions and other unauthorised conduct

Often employees are expressly forbidden from engaging in certain activities during work. For example, a factory operative may be forbidden from consuming alcohol. Does the employee's failure to comply with his employer's instructions take the employee outwith the scope of his employment? The general rule is that if the express prohibition sets a limit to the work which the employee is authorised to do, the employee acts outwith the scope of his employment. However, if the employee is simply doing what he is authorised to do in an unauthorised way, he remains within the scope of his employment. For example, in *McKean* v *Raynor Bros Ltd* (1942) a workman was employed by the defendants. He was instructed by the latter to take a lorry, and meet and give a message to a convoy which was coming by road. He proceeded on his journey, but instead of taking the firm's lorry, he used his father's car. He drove the car negligently and collided with, and killed, the claimant's husband. It was held that the workman was doing what he was authorised to do in an unauthorised way. His employer was, therefore, vicariously liable for his conduct.

## Acts intended to benefit employer

If the employee's conduct is motivated by his desire to assist his employer, the courts will be inclined to construe such conduct as being within the scope of his employment provided that the act in question is reasonably incidental to that which the employee is employed to do. For example, in *Baird* v *Graham* (1852) an employer sent his servant with a horse to a fair. The servant had to put the horses up for the night. He did so in premises which were occupied by the pursuer. Unfortunately, the pursuer's horses became infected by disease which was transmitted by the horse which the servant was in charge of. It was held that the employer was liable.

Again, in *Mulholland* v *William Reid and Leys Ltd* (1958) the pursuer was killed at work by one of his employer's vans which was being driven by an apprentice who had no driving licence, and was not an authorised driver. Prior to driving the van, he and another apprentice had been assisting a tradesman to move a piece of equipment into a workshop by hand. The way had been blocked by a van. The apprentice had not been instructed to drive a van but, nonetheless, he did so and in so doing killed a fellow employee. It was held that, whereas the conduct of the apprentice had not been authorised, it was sufficiently incidental to the work which he had to do, to bring the negligent conduct within the scope of his employment. The apprentice was simply doing what he was employed to do, in an unauthorised way. The defenders were, therefore, liable.

## Assaults

The general rule is that an employer will not be liable for an assault which is perpetrated by an employee, if the employee is solely motivated by spite against the person who is assaulted: *Warren* v *Henly's Ltd* (1948). However, an employer will be vicariously liable for the assault by his employee, if the assault is carried out in furtherance of the business of the employer: *Daniels* v *Whetstone Entertainments* (1962). Again, in *Mattis* v *Pollock* (2003) the defendant (P) owned a night club. He employed X as a doorman. X was expected to act aggressively towards customers. One night, X grabbed a member of a group of people who were about to enter the nightclub. X was struck several times and also hit by a bottle. X then escaped to his flat from which he emerged with a knife, and stabbed M, who was seriously injured as a result. It was held that P was vicariously liable for the assault, since X's act was so closely connected with what P either authorised, or expected of X, that it was fair, just and reasonable to make P vicariously liable for the assault.

*Fennelly* v *Connex South Eastern Ltd* (2000) is an interesting case on the issue as to whether the employee is acting within the course of his employment. In that case the claimant, C, alleged that one of the defendants' employees, (S), a ticket inspector, had assaulted him at a railway station, in the course of the latter's employment. The claimant had purchased a ticket, and had passed through the ticket barrier. As he made his way down the steps towards the platform, S called after him and asked to see his railway ticket. However, C did not stop. There was an altercation, during which C was offensive to S. C then walked away. S then put C in a headlock and ejected him from the station. At first instance the judge held that S had ceased to carry out his authorised role and started pursuing his own ends, when C walked away and S became personally angry. S was therefore not acting within the course of his employment when he assaulted C. However, the Court of Appeal held that whether a given act was carried out in the course of the employment of the person who perpetrated the attack, it was necessary to look at the job in question, and not divide out each step and task which was authorised by the employer. The initial altercation occurred as a result of S's job as a ticket inspector. The assault followed from that altercation.

It was artificial to say that simply because C was walking away when the assault took place, what happened during the assault was divorced from what preceded it. In the last analysis, the assault took place during the course of S's employment. The defendants were, therefore, liable.

The leading case concerning vicarious liability for assaults which have been perpetrated by employees is now *Lister* v *Hesley Hall Ltd* (2001). The claimant was a resident in a boarding house which was attached to a school which was owned and managed by the defendants. The warden of the boarding house, who was employed by the defendants, without their knowledge, systematically sexually abused the claimant, who sued the defendants on the basis that the harm which had been inflicted on him was done within the scope of the warden's employment, thus rendering the defendants vicariously liable for the assault. The House of Lords, in finding in favour of the claimant, held that there was sufficient connection between the work which the warden was employed to do, and the acts of abuse which he had committed against the claimant, for those acts to fall within the scope of his employment. Furthermore, it was quite irrelevant that the warden had acted both illegally, and also for his own personal gratification.

The issue of vicarious liability of an employer for assaults which are committed by his employee was considered by the Court of Appeal in *Maga* v *Archbishop of Birmingham* (2010). In that case the claimant, who had learning difficulties, brought an action against a Roman Catholic diocese. The claimant alleged that he had been sexually abused by a priest who worked in the diocese. The claimant was not a Roman Catholic. He had met the priest, who had special responsibility for youth work, through church discos. The court held the diocese vicariously liable for the conduct of the priest. There was a sufficiently close connection between that which the priest was employed to and the abuse in question. In reaching this decision, the court took into account the following factors:

(1) The priest was usually dressed in clerical garb, and was so dressed when he had met the claimant.

(2) The priest's duties included a duty to evangelise or bring the gospel to both Catholics and non-Catholics.

(3) At the time the abuse took place, the priest was carrying out one of his specifically assigned functions in the church.

(4) The priest was both able to develop and did develop his relationship with the claimant by inviting him to a disco which was held on church premises and which was organised by the priest.

(5) The relationship between the priest and the claimant was further developed by the priest getting the claimant to help clear up after discos.

(6) The claimant worked at the request of the priest on premises which were owned by the priest's archdiocese. The premises also adjoined the church where the priest worked.

(7) The opportunity to spend time alone with the claimant, especially in the presbytery, arose from the priest's role in the archdiocese.

The Court of Appeal case of *E* v *English Province of Our Lady of Charity* (2012) also concerned alleged sexual abuse by a priest. However, whereas in *Maga* it was admitted that, for the purposes of that action, the priest who allegedly abused the claimant was employed by the relevant Roman Catholic archdiocese, in *E*, both parties to the action accepted the fact that the relevant priest was not employed by his diocese. The sole question which fell to be answered was whether the defendant diocese was vicariously liable for the alleged sexual abuse of the priest. The court held that, whereas the priest was not employed by the defendant diocese, the relationship between the diocese and the priest was akin to that between employer and employee, that it was fair and just to make the diocese vicariously liable for the conduct of the priest. In holding the defendant vicariously liable for the conduct of the priest, the court took into account that the alleged abuse was close to the nature of his appointment. Furthermore, the very empowerment of the priest by the bishop materially increased the risk of an assault being carried out by the former.

Whereas in both *Maga* and also *E*, the defendant was a diocese, in the Supreme Court case of *Various Claimants* v *Institute of the Brothers of the Christian Schools* (2012) the defendant was an unincorporated organisation. Here, the victims were allegedly sexually and physically abused by brothers (who were members of the defendant organisation) while the claimants were pupils at a residential school. The Supreme Court was required to decide whether the defendant was vicariously liable for the alleged abuse which was perpetrated by the brothers. The brothers who taught at the school were not contractually employed by the defendant. The Supreme Court was of the view that one was required to adopt a two-staged test in determining whether the defendant was liable. The first stage was to decide whether the relationship between the defendant and the brothers was akin to that of employer and employee. The court answered this in the affirmative. The second stage comprised answering the question as to whether the acts of abuse were sufficiently closely connected to the relationship between the brothers and the defendant, to render the latter vicariously liable for such acts in tort. Again, the court answered this question in the affirmative. The boy victims lived in a cloistered environment. They were virtual prisoners in the school. They were doubly vulnerable because their personal history was such that it rendered disclosure of potential abuse less likely than would have been the case otherwise. Whereas, in effect, the act of abusing the boys who were in the care of the brothers was the antithesis of the objectives of the organisation (which was to care for the educational and religious needs of pupils), in the opinion of the court, that very fact was one of the factors which provided the necessary close connection between the alleged abuse and the relationship between the brothers and the defendant in order to give rise to vicarious liability on the part of the latter. It was fair, just and reasonable to hold the defendant liable.

The potential liability of an unincorporated organisation for assaults which have been committed by members of the organisation fell to be determined again in *A v The Trustees of the Watchtower Bible and Tract Society* (2015). In this case, the claimant claimed that the defendant, a society of Jehovah's Witnesses (an unincorporated body), was vicariously liable for a series of sexual assaults which had been perpetrated by a ministerial servant, S, of the defendant, when the claimant was a child. The Jehovah's witnesses are organised on a hierarchical basis. The governing body supervises over 100 branches worldwide, each of which is supervised by a branch committee. One of the branch offices is in London. The branch committee there oversees districts within the branch, and also assigns a district overseer to oversee each district. Within each district there are about twelve circuits. A circuit overseer is assigned to each circuit. Within each circuit there are about twenty congregations. Within each congregation there are elders, ministerial servants and members of the congregation. However, whereas the Jehovah's Witnesses are organised on a hierarchical basis, there is no hierarchical structure which sets apart a clergy class from the laity. All members are expected to teach and can lead in Bible study. Congregational responsibilities are split between elders and ministerial servants. The primary role of the elder is to guide and protect the congregation spiritually etc. The main role of ministerial servants is to provide practical assistance to the elders and service to the congregation. Whereas Globe J accepted the fact that ministerial servants generally did not have any formal pastoring or shepherding role, they could be used in such a capacity if there were insufficient elders. The defendants accepted the fact that S had sexually abused the claimant.

The crucial issue to be determined by the court was where the assaults took place and what activities were taking place when the assaults were committed.

In order to ascertain if the defendants were vicariously liable for the assaults which had been committed by S upon the claimant, Globe J drew on the learning in *E* and *Various Claimants*. A two-staged test, therefore, fell to be applied. As far as the first stage was concerned, the relationship between a ministerial servant and the Jehovah's Witnesses was sufficiently close to one of employer–employee that it was fair and just to impose vicarious liability. As far as the application of the second stage was concerned, the progressive acts of intimacy which had been perpetrated by S were only possible because he had the actual, or ostensible authority of a ministerial servant that meant that no one questioned his being alone with the claimant. Thus, there was a close connection between the abuse and what S was authorised to do. In the last analysis, it was fair and just to hold the defendants vicariously liable for his acts.

The claimant also claimed, not only that the defendants were vicariously liable for S's conduct, but also that the elders owed her a direct duty of care to safeguard her from harm. The claimant asserted that after the elders had become aware that S had assaulted another child, the elders assumed responsibility to the claimant to protect her from harm. Globe J held that the elders had assumed such a responsibility, in that they had appreciated the risks S posed to children in the future. Thus, there was a sufficient relationship of proximity between the elders and the children of members to protect the children from sexual abuse by S. In the opinion of his Lordship, there was an assumption of a responsibility on the part of the elders to warn both the congregation and individual parents about the risks which were posed by S. The scope of the duty of care which was owed was to warn the congregation and individual parents about the risks which were posed by S.

The application of the two-staged test by the courts, in order to ascertain whether an employer is vicariously liable for assaults which have been perpetrated by employees, is illustrated in the Inner House case of *Vaickuviene* v *J Sainsbury plc* (2013). The pursuers were the relatives of V who had been murdered by a co-employee (M) in the defenders' supermarket. M was a member of the British National Party. He had extreme racist views. V was Eastern European. M had informed V that the former did not like immigrants. Several days before the murder took place, M informed V that he would murder him. The pursuers claimed that the defenders were vicariously liable for the delictual conduct of M in terms of s 8 of the Protection from Harassment Act 1997. Since M had been employed by the defenders at the time the murder took place, one had simply to determine whether M's actions were so closely connected with what he was employed to do, that they could be seen as ways of carrying out the work which he was authorised to do. M was employed to stack shelves in retail premises. There was no connection between stacking shelves and the harassment or murder of V. In the last analysis, M's employment had simply provided him with an opportunity to carry out his own personal campaign of harassment against V. See also *Wilson* v *Exel UK Ltd* (2010) and *Graham* v *Commercial Bodyworks Ltd* (2015).

The Supreme Court had the opportunity to review the law relating to vicarious liability for assaults which have been perpetrated by employees in *Mohamud* v *WM Morrison Supermarkets plc* (2016). In that case the claimant, M, entered the defendants' premises which included a petrol station and a kiosk where customers pay for their purchases. M requested K, who was employed by the defendants to see that the petrol pumps were kept in good order and serve customers, if M could print some documents from a USB stick. K responded in foul, racist and abusive language and ordered M to leave, and never return. K then followed M to the latter's car, where the former assaulted the latter. Both the trial judge and the Court of Appeal held that K's assaulting M was insufficiently closely connected to K's employment to make the defendant vicariously liable for his conduct. M successfully appealed to the Supreme Court. The court expressed the view that in deciding whether the defendant was vicariously liable for the conduct of another, first, there required to be a relationship between the defendant and the other. Since in the instant case K had been employed by the defendants, there was no issue on that point. Second, one was required to determine whether there was a sufficient connection between that relationship and the wrongdoer's act or default. In deciding this issue the court endorsed the "close connection" test which had been affirmed many times. In applying this test one had to consider two matters. The first was what functions, or field of activities, had been entrusted by the employer to the employee? In short, what was the nature of the latter's job? That question had to be addressed broadly. The second question one had to answer was whether there was a sufficient connection between the position for which the employee was employed, that would make it just to make the employer vicariously liable for the misconduct of his employee. In the instant case, K had been employed to attend to customers, and to respond to their enquiries. Whilst his foul–mouthed and abusive response to M's request was inexcusable, it was within the scope of his employment. What happened thereafter constituted an unbroken sequence of events. First, it was not right to regard K as having (metaphorically) taken off his uniform the moment he stepped from behind the counter. K was simply following up what he had said to M. It was a seamless episode. Second, when K followed M back to the car, K had told M never to return to the defendant's petrol station. That was not something which was personal between them. It was an order to keep away from his employer's premises which he reinforced by violence. K was purporting to act about his employer's business. Whilst K had grossly abused his position, such an order was in connection with the business by which he was employed to serve customers. The defendants had entrusted K with that position and it was just that as between the defendants and M, the defendants should be held responsible for K's abuse of that position.

Whereas the above cases have all centred round the potential liability of employers, and others, for assaults which have been carried out by employees and other persons, the Supreme Court had the opportunity to decide whether the learning, which had been generated by the above assault cases, was applicable in a context where the harm which had been inflicted by an employee was done by way of his negligence. The facts in *Cox* v *Ministry of Justice* (2016) were simple. Whilst working in the prison kitchen, a prisoner accidentally dropped a sack of rice on the back of an employee who worked in the kitchen. She was injured as a result. The court was required to determine whether the prison service was vicariously liable for the harm which had been caused by the prisoner. The court, in essence, was required to decide whether the defendants were vicariously liable for the negligent conduct of someone who was not employed by the former, but performed functions on their behalf. The court refused to set store by the fact that the defendants were carrying out a business or a commercial enterprise. Rather, it sufficed for vicarious liability to lie that the defendant was carrying on activities in the furtherance of its own interests, and the individual who performed the tortious (or delictual) act was carrying out activities which had been assigned to him by the defendant, as an integral part of its operations for its benefit. In the instant case, the prisoner, who was working in the prison kitchen was integrated in the operation of the prison. The activities which were assigned to the prisoner formed an integral part of the activities which it carried on in furtherance of its aims, in particular, the activity of providing meals for prisoners. A prisoner performing such activities is placed in a position where there is a risk that he may perform a negligent act within the field of activities which were assigned to him. The fact that the prison service and the operators of contracted-out prisons were performing a statutory duty in providing prisoners with useful work was not incompatible with the imposition of vicarious liability. In the last analysis, the defendants were vicariously liable for the harm which had been caused by the negligent act of the prisoner.

## Thefts

To what extent, if any, is an employer vicariously liable for his employee stealing goods which the pursuer had deposited with the employer? Could the employer claim that such conduct on the part of the employee is not committed within the scope of the employment of the latter, since the employee is not employed to steal such goods? The leading case on the subject is *Brink's Global Services Inc* v *Igrox Ltd* (2010). Here, the claimants provided a worldwide door-to-door service for the carriage of goods. The claimants entered into a contract with a London bank to convey silver bars to India. The bars were packed in wooden pallets which were required to be fumigated, in order to reduce the risk of infestation. The claimants, therefore, entered into a contract with the defendants, whereby the latter undertook to fumigate the pallets. An employee of the defendants was given the task of fumigating the pallets which were stored in a container. He entered the container and stole some silver bars, which were never returned. The defendants were held vicariously liable for the theft. The Court of Appeal held that there was a sufficiently close connection between the employee's theft of the silver and the purpose of his employment to make it fair and just that the defendants should be vicariously liable for his actions. The theft by an employee from the very container which he was instructed to fumigate was a risk which was reasonably incidental to the purpose for which he was employed.

## Fraud

Fraud is a delict in the law of Scotland. The gist of the wrong is that the defender has, by his dishonest word or deed, deliberately persuaded the pursuer to act to his detriment (*Bradford Third Equitable Benefit Society* v *Borders*). Falsity is the very foundation of the delict. In the House of Lords case of *Derry* v *Peek* (1889) Lord Herschell stated that fraud is proved when it is shown that a false representation has been made:

(1) knowingly; or

(2) without belief in its truth; or

(3) recklessly, careless whether it be true or false.

The leading case on vicarious liability of an employer for the fraud of his employee is *Lloyd* v *Grace Smith and Co Ltd* (1912). Here, a solicitor's clerk fraudulently persuaded the claimant to transfer her property to him. The employer was held liable for this act of fraud. The House of Lords held that his fraudulent act fell within the scope of his employment. Furthermore it was quite irrelevant that the employee had simply acted for his own benefit, in contrast to that of his employer. More recently, in *Dubai Aluminium Co Ltd* v *Salaam* (2003) a partner in a firm of solicitors dishonestly drafted an agreement, the result of which was that the claimants were defrauded. The House of Lords, in deciding that the defendants were liable, held that the acts of fraud were so closely connected with what the partner was authorised to do that such acts could fairly be regarded as done by him in the ordinary course of the firm's business.

## Lending a servant

It sometimes happens that X, who is an employee of A, is hired by B in order to perform some task for the latter and, during the time when X is working for B, X negligently injures P. To what extent, if any, would either A or B be vicariously liable for the conduct of X?

Generally, the law imposes a strong presumption against the person who borrows a servant being held vicariously liable for the conduct of the servant while he is performing tasks for the hirer (*Malley* v *LMS Railway Co*). The leading case on the subject is now *Mersey Docks and Harbour Board* v *Coggins and Griffith* (1947). In that case, a harbour authority lent a mobile crane to the defendant firm of stevedores for loading a ship. A craneman, X, was also lent by the authority. He was paid by the authority and he was also liable to be dismissed by it. The contract between the authority and the stevedores stipulated that cranemen who were hired, should be deemed to be employees of the hirers. While X was carrying out work for the defendants, X injured the claimant who sued the harbour authority for damages. The House of Lords held the harbour authority liable since, in the eyes of the law, the harbour authority had continued to employ X throughout the duration of the period while he was working for the stevedores. The House of Lords expressed the view that, in circumstances where an employee is borrowed by another party, there is a strong presumption that the employee remains the employee of the lender. Importantly, the House stated that the provisions of the relevant contract between the parties which governed who was to be regarded as the employer of the worker concerned, were not to be regarded as conclusive as to who was to be deemed liable for any injury which was caused to a third party.

## Unauthorised lifts

Commonly, employees are forbidden from giving a lift to others in vehicles which belong to their employers. However, if in the face of such a prohibition, the employee does give someone a lift in his employer's vehicle and proceeds to drive negligently, the result of which is that the vehicle is involved in an accident and the passenger is injured, would the driver's employer be vicariously liable for the negligent conduct of the employee? In *Peebles* v *Cowan and Co* (1915) a driver allowed a boy to ride on a horse-drawn lorry. The boy fell off and was injured. It was held that by giving the boy permission to ride on the lorry, the employee was acting outwith the scope of his employment. His employers were not, therefore, vicariously liable for the injury which the boy had sustained.

The English courts have sometimes categorised unauthorised passengers as trespassers *vis à vis* the employer, in order to preclude liability on the part of the latter (see, eg, *Twine* v *Beans Express Ltd*). However, to what extent such an approach represents the law of Scotland is uncertain. There is little authority on this point.

More recently, the issue of liability of employers for accidents which involved unauthorised lifts, fell to be considered in the Court of Appeal case of *Rose* v *Plenty* (1976). In that case, the employers of a milk float driver, X, had prohibited him from allowing boys to assist the driver in delivering milk. X, however, flouted this instruction and allowed the claimant youth to assist him delivering milk one day. X drove the milk float negligently. The claimant was injured. The court held that since the claimant had been allowed to ride on the float, in order to assist the driver in delivering milk, the driver was simply doing what he was authorised to do in an unauthorised way. In the last analysis, the employer was liable.

## Liability for acts of independent contractors

We now turn our attention to the extent to which an employer is liable for the acts of an independent contractor. The general rule is that an employer is not liable for the acts of an independent contractor. Therefore, I am not liable in the law of delict if the taxi driver whom I pay to drive me to the railway station, negligently collides with another vehicle during the course of the journey. However, there are certain situations where an employer will be held vicariously liable for the conduct of an independent contractor. The list of categories of the activities where the courts have held an employer liable for the acts of an independent contractor (which we will now look at) is not closed.

### Employer at fault

If the employer is at fault in same way for the injury in question, the employer would be liable. For example, if I employ a building contractor who is patently unsuited to carrying out the work which I have commissioned him to perform, and during the course of carrying out the work he injures the pursuer, I would be vicariously liable in the law of delict. The employer would also be liable if he fails to give an independent contractor adequate instructions as to how the latter should carry out his duties (see, eg, *Robinson* v *Beaconsfield RDC*).

### The performance of non-delegable duties

The law places an employer under a non-delegable duty to third parties in certain circumstances. In short, the law will not allow an employer to transfer any duty which the law imposes on him, to the person whom he has commissioned to carry out the relevant task.

### Acts which derogate from the right and support of land

If A employs an independent contractor, X, who, in the course of carrying out work on A's land, causes subsidence or loss of support on adjoining premises which belongs to B, who is entitled to the support which is afforded by A's premises, then A is liable for the harm which is caused to B's property. In the Inner House case of *Stewart* v *Malik* (2009) the proprietors of a flat, which was situated in a tenement, brought an action for damages against the defenders who were proprietors of a shop which was situated immediately below the flat. The relevant damage had been caused by the removal of a load-bearing wall, during the course of works which were being carried out in the shop. The court held that since, in Scotland, the law of the tenement casts on the servient proprietor a positive duty, in carrying out works which may affect support, to avoid endangering the dominant property, such a duty could not be displaced by the servient proprietor commissioning an independent contractor to carry out the works in question. Therefore, the defenders were liable for the damage which had been caused by the independent contractor.

## Extra-hazardous acts

It is well established in English law that if A commissions an independent contractor to carry out works which are intrinsically hazardous, the law will impose strict liability on A for any damage which is caused by the contractor. For example, in *Honeywill and Stein* v *Larkin Bros* (1934) an independent contractor was employed to take flashlight photographs in a cinema. During the course of taking photographs, curtains in the cinema caught fire, and damage was caused to the cinema. The Court of Appeal held that since the activity in question was inherently dangerous, the party who had commissioned him to take the photographs was vicariously liable for the damage which the contractor had caused.

However, in *Biffa Waste Services Ltd* v *Maschininenfrabrok Ernst Hese GmbH* (2009) Stanley Burnton LJ expressed the view that the doctrine of vicarious liability for the performance of extra-hazardous activities was so unsatisfactory that it should be kept within narrow limits. To what extent the doctrine is recognised by the law of Scotland is uncertain. In *Stewart* v *Malik* the Lord President reserved his opinion as to whether an employer was liable for harm which had been caused by an independent contractor while he was carrying out extra-hazardous operations. In the Outer House case of *McManus* v *City Link Development Ltd* (2015) Lord Jones, in effect, also reserved his opinion as to whether Scots law recognised such a form of vicarious liability.

## Employer retains full control over independent contractor

There is authority for the proposition that an employer is liable for the negligence of an independent contractor if the former continues to exercise a significant degree of control over the latter at the time the accident takes place (see, for example, *Steven* v *Thurso Commissioners of Police* (1876)).

## Non-delegable legal duties

An employer cannot delegate certain duties which the law imposes on him to an agent, thereby absolving himself from delictual liability should the latter injure a third party in discharging his duties. For example, in *Wilsons and Clyde Coal Co* v *English* (1938) the House of Lords held that the duty which the common law imposed on an employer to maintain a safe system of work, could not be delegated to an agent. The employer was, therefore, liable for the injury which a miner sustained as a result of such a system not being maintained by its agent.

A more recent example of the courts deciding that a duty is non-delegable is seen in the Supreme Court case of *Woodland* v *Swimming Teachers*

*Association* (2013). In that case, a pupil of a school in the local education authority's area suffered a severe brain injury during a swimming lesson which had been arranged by the school at a pool which was run by another local authority. The lesson was supervised by a swimming teacher and a life guard, both of whom were employed by an independent contractor who organised and provided the lesson. The claimant brought a personal injury claim against, *inter alia*, the contractor, the life guard and the two local authorities. The claimant alleged that the education authority owed her a non-delegable duty to secure that reasonable care was taken of the claimant during the school day when she was at a separate location from the school. The court in overturning the decision of the Court of Appeal (in a striking out action) held that the school owed a duty towards a vulnerable claimant for the purpose of performing a function for which the defendant had assumed responsibility, and that, within school hours, a school was in such a position of responsibility and control over a pupil, and therefore it was fair, just and reasonable to hold a school liable for injury which had been caused by the negligence of an independent contractor to whom it had delegated its educational function and control over a pupil during the school day.

In reaching its decision in favour of the claimant, the court drew attention to the fact that the boundaries of vicarious liability had been expanded by recent decisions to embrace tortfeasors who were not employees of the defendant but, notwithstanding that fact, stood in a relationship which was analogous to employment. However, the principle had never extended liability to embrace liability for the negligence of a truly independent contractor, as was the independent contractor in the instant case. In the instant case, the defendant local authority had assumed a duty to ensure that the claimant's swimming lessons were carefully conducted and supervised by whomever they might get to perform these functions. Furthermore, swimming lessons were an integral part of the school's teaching function. The very act of negligence on the part of the independent contractor occurred in the course of the very functions which the school had assumed an obligation to perform and delegated to its contractors. It therefore followed that if the latter were negligent in performing its duties and the claimant was injured, the defendant was in breach of its duty. The court also drew attention to the fact that the imposition of a non-delegable duty on schools in such circumstances would not impose an unreasonable financial burden on them.

Furthermore, if statute, in contrast to the common law, imposes an absolute duty on an employer to perform a particular task the employer remains liable if the duty is negligently discharged by an independent contractor: *Robinson* v *Beaconsfield RDC* (1911).

## Operations affecting the highway (road)

Where an employer commissions an independent contractor to carry out work, either on, or adjoining a road, such work being of a potentially dangerous nature, the employer remains liable, should the contractor carry out the work negligently. For example, in *Tarry v Ashton* (1876) the defendant employed an independent contractor to repair a lamp which was attached to his house. The lamp, which overhung a footpath which adjoined the road, was not securely fastened, the upshot of which was that the lamp fell and injured the plaintiff. It was held that the employer was liable for the contractor's negligence.

## No liability for collateral acts of negligence

An employer is not liable for the collateral acts of negligence of an independent contractor. In other words, an employer is not liable for acts which the contractor performs which are extrinsic to the task which the contractor has been commissioned to perform. For example, in *Padbury v Holliday and Greenwood Ltd* (1912) an independent contractor was employed to fit casement windows in a building. A workman negligently placed a tool on the sill of the window on which he was working at the time. The wind blew the window open. The tool was knocked off the window sill. A passerby was injured as a consequence. The Court of Appeal held that the employer was not liable for this injury, since the tool in question had not been placed on the sill during the ordinary course of work. In the last analysis, there was nothing really inherently dangerous in the work which the contractor was employed to perform. Rather, it was the manner in which the work was performed which created the danger.

## Lending a car

Here we consider the extent, if any, the owner of a vehicle is liable for the injury which is caused by someone else driving the vehicle in a negligent manner. The leading case is *Morgans v Launchbury* (1973). In that case, the defendant owned a car. She lent it to her husband who took it on a pub crawl. He drank too much alcohol, with the result that he could not drive safely. He, therefore, asked his drinking companion to drive the car. His companion did so negligently, and injured the plaintiff. The House of Lords held that the defendant car owner was not liable for the harm which the claimant sustained since, for liability to lie, it was essential that the car was being used for the purposes of the owner, under the delegation of a task or duty.

For liability to lie it is also necessary that the driver of the vehicle is using the vehicle for a specific purpose on behalf of the owner. This point is illustrated in the Court of Appeal case of *Norwood* v *Navan* (1981). A husband allowed his wife to use his car. She often used the car in order to go shopping. One day, the wife went on a shopping expedition with friends. She drove the car negligently and injured the claimant. It was held that the husband was not vicariously liable for his wife's negligence since, at the time the accident took place, she was not carrying out a particular task at the behest of her husband. It was insufficient that he simply knew that the car could be used for family shopping when the wife chose to do so.

## Essential Facts

- An employer can be sued for delicts which have been committed by his employee during the course of the latter's employment.
- An employer is not normally vicariously liable for the delictual conduct of an independent contractor.
- The courts employ a number of tests in order to distinguish an employee from an independent contractor.
- An employee is employed under a contract of service whereas an independent contractor is employed under a contract for services.
- It is a question of law whether a person is employed under a contract of service or a contract of services.
- The courts adopt a variety of tests to distinguish a contract of service from a contract for services, namely whether one has the right to choose who works for him, the payment of wages, the right to control the other and, the right to hire and fire.
- An employer is liable only for acts which are done in the course of employment of the employee.
- An employer is not liable if the employee has gone on a frolic of his own.
- If an employee has deviated substantially from the normal or authorised journey the employer will not be liable.
- If employee is doing what he is authorised to do, albeit in an incompetent manner, the employer is still liable.
- If the employee performing an act which is reasonably incidental to what he is employed to do, the employer will be liable.
- The employer will not be liable for an assault which is perpetrated by an employee who is motivated by spite.
- In certain limited circumstances an employer is liable for the acts of an independent contractor, namely when the employer is himself at fault; and when the law imposes on the employer a non-delegable duty.

## Essential Cases

**Bell v Blackwood, Morton and Sons (1960)**: an employer will be liable for the conduct of his employee at the relevant place of employment during the hours for which the employee is employed, and also as long as the employee is on the premises concerned, within reasonable limits of time of the commencement and conclusion of the shift.

**Storey v Ashton (1869)**: no liability if employee has gone on a frolic of his own. A cart driver went to visit a relative and injured P in the process. Held that the employer was not liable.

**Lister v Hesley Hall Ltd (2001)**: a warden in a special boarding school systematically sexually abused a child in his care. Held that there was sufficient connection between the work which the warden had been paid to do and the acts he committed to make his employers vicariously liable for his conduct.

**Mattis v Pollock (2003)**: an employer will be liable for the assault of his employee if the assault is carried out in furtherance of his employer's business.

**Various Claimants v Institute of the Christian Schools (2012)**: unincorporated religious organisation held vicariously liable for assaults perpetrated against children who were residents at a school where members of the organisation taught. Two-staged test was applied. The relationship between the brothers who committed the assault and the defendant was akin to that of employer and employee. Second, the acts of abuse were sufficiently closely connected to that relationship to render the defendant liable.

**Mohamud v WM Morrison Supermarkets plc (2016)**: M assaulted by K who was employed by the defendant to serve customers and look after the petrol pumps at a filling station which was situated on D's premises. Prior to committing the assault K had racially abused M and had told M never to return to the premises. Held, the whole sequence of events leading up to and including the actual assault should not be regarded as comprising discrete phases, independent of each other. Rather, one should regard one as a continuation of the other. Looked at *in toto* they were sufficiently closely connected to what K was employed to do to render the defendant vicariously liable for the assault.

**Cox v Ministry of Justice (2016)**: prisoner working in prison kitchen negligently injures employee of defendant. Held, prisoner's work formed integral part of the operation of the prison. The prisoner had been placed in a situation where there was a risk he could perform a negligent act. The defendants were, therefore, vicariously liable for the injury which the employee had sustained.

# 11 DEFENCES

When looking at delicts, such as the law of nuisance and defamation, we saw that there were particular defences which were associated with these delicts. In this chapter we look at defences which apply *generally* in the law of delict.

## CONTRIBUTORY NEGLIGENCE

Section 1(1) of the Law Reform (Contributory Negligence) Act 1945 provides:

> "Where a person suffers damage as a result partly of his own fault and partly of the fault of another person, or persons, a claim in respect of that damage shall not be defeated by reason of the fault of the person suffering the damage, but the damages recoverable in respect thereof shall be reduced to such an extent as the court thinks just and equitable having regard to the claimant's share and responsibility for the damage."

Essentially, the Act provides that a claim should not fail completely because the pursuer is in some way to blame for his or her injuries.

Under s 4, "damage" includes loss of life and personal injury. "Fault" means negligence, breach of statutory duty or other omission which gives rise to a liability in tort or would, apart from the Act, give rise to the defence of contributory negligence. The Act is inapplicable in relation to acts of dishonesty: *Corporacion Nacional de Chile* v *Sogemin Metals Ltd* (1997). The Act may be applicable to cases of assault: *Murphy* v *Culhane* (1977).

There are no clearly defined rules to determine what conduct on the part of the pursuer ranks as "just and equitable". Some authors have argued that the pursuer requires to be morally culpable in some way for the defence to operate. In *Quintas* v *National Smelting Co* (1961) Sellers LJ stated:

> "The respective responsibilities of the parties, and what is just and equitable having regard thereto can only properly be assessed when it has been found what the plaintiff in fact did and what the defendants failed in their duty to do."

The court determines what the total amount of damages would be if the pursuer had not been at fault and then apportions liability as a percentage of the total. If there is more than one defender liability will be apportioned between them depending upon their respective blameworthiness. For example, in *Davies* v *Swan Motor Company Ltd* (1949) a bus ran into a lorry. Davies was killed. Both the bus driver and the lorry driver were at fault. Davies himself had been partly to blame for his injury, in that when the accident took place he had been standing on the lorry sidestep contrary to instructions. It was held that Davies own negligence had contributed to his death. Damages were therefore reduced by one-fifth. The bus driver was held responsible for two-thirds of the remainder, and the lorry driver responsible for the remaining one-third. Appellate courts are generally reluctant to overturn a judge's decision as to how liability should be apportioned between parties: *Porter* v *Strathclyde Regional Council* (1991). However, the Supreme Court case of *Jackson* v *Murray* (2015) provides a good example, that in certain circumstances, an appellate court is prepared to do so. In that case, the pursuer raised an action for damages in respect of injuries which she received as a result of being struck by a motor vehicle which was being driven by the defender, after the pursuer had alighted from a school bus. The Lord Ordinary found the defender liable in negligence. However, he found the pursuer had been contributorily negligent and reduced damages accordingly. The pursuer reclaimed against the decision to the Inner House which reduced the assessment of contributory negligence to 70 per cent. The pursuer then appealed to the Supreme Court which decided that the appellant should be awarded 50 per cent damages.

The 1945 Act is not confined to acts of contributory "negligence". The Act also applies to a situation where the pursuer intends to do injury to himself. In *Reeves* v *Metropolitan Police Commissioner* (2000) the claimant, who was sane at the time, committed suicide while in police custody. The House of Lords held that while defendants owed the claimant a duty of care to take reasonable measures to prevent him from harming himself, damages which were awarded to him fell to be reduced by 50 per cent.

### Pursuer must contribute to damage

For the defence of contributory negligence to apply, it is essential that the pursuer's conduct contributes to the damage he sustains. For example, there may be reduction in damages where a motorcyclist fails to wear a crash helmet (*O'Connell* v *Jackson* (1972)) or where a car passenger fails to wear his seat belt (*Froom* v *Butcher* (1976)).

The pursuer need not owe the defender a duty of care for the defence to succeed: *Davies*. However, the pursuer requires to be able to foresee risk to himself, and the consequences of his failing to take the relevant prophylactic action. In *Jones* v *Livox Quarries Ltd* (1952) the claimant was riding on the tow bar of a traxcavator (a vehicle used to carry stones). There was, of course, an obvious danger of his being thrown off the vehicle. However, he was hit by a vehicle which approached from behind him. He was injured. It was claimed, on his behalf, that he had not contributed to his injury. However, the Court of Appeal held that the damages which were awarded to him fell to be reduced under the Act, on account of his contributory negligence in that he ought reasonably to have foreseen that if he did not act as a reasonably prudent man, he might himself be hurt.

## Standard of care

The standard of care which applies to the defence of contributory negligence is the same as that applying generally in the law of negligence: *Billing* v *Riden* (1958). See also *Porter* v *Strathclyde RC* (1991). However, concessions are made to children. In the Privy Council case of *Yachuk* v *Oliver Blais Co Ltd* (1949) the defendant supplied the plaintiff (aged 9) with petrol. The latter used the petrol to play a game. He was badly burned. It was held that there was no contributory negligence on the part of the plaintiff, since a normal child of his age could not be expected to know the properties of petrol. In *Gough* v *Thorne* (1996) a girl aged 13 was beckoned to cross a road by a lorry driver who had stopped his vehicle. She was hit by a car which overtook the lorry on the inside of the road. The Court of Appeal held that she had not been contributorily negligent, in that she had behaved as any other child of her age would do in the circumstances.

## Agony of "moment rule"

There is no contributory negligence if the defender has put the pursuer in a dangerous situation, and damage accrues to the pursuer by virtue of him trying to extricate himself from that situation. In *Jones* v *Boyce* (1816) the claimant was a passenger on a coach. The coach was in danger of overturning. He jumped off the coach. It was held that there was no contributory negligence on his part. However, if the pursuer is simply threatened with personal inconvenience of a trifling kind, he is not entitled to take unreasonable risks: *Adams* v *London and York Railway* (1869).

## Defence to be pled

The defence of contributory negligence must be specifically pled: *Porter* v *Strathclyde RC* (1991). The defender must go on to prove that the pursuer was at fault.

# CONSENT

The defence of consent is often expressed by the Latin maxim *volenti non fit iniuria*, that is to say: no wrong is done to he who has consented. Where a person consents to run the risk of injury, he cannot, thereafter, claim damages in respect of the injury caused by the risk. The defence must be specifically pled. The onus of proof that the pursuer was *volenti* rests on the defender. The defence operates as a complete defence.

## Nature of the defence

"It is essential before a plea of *volenti non fit injuria* could be upheld, that there should be relevant averments not only to the effect that the pursuer knew of the risk of danger, but also that he voluntarily agreed to take the risk on himself.": *Kirkham* v *Cementation Co Ltd* (1964).

For the defence to apply, the defender requires to prove that the pursuer, with full knowledge of the nature and extent of the risk he ran, freely and voluntarily agreed to incur it. In other words, the pursuer must be both *sciens* and *volens*. In *Nettleship* v *Weston* (1971) Lord Denning MR stated:

> "Knowledge of the risk of injury is not enough. Nor is a willingness to take the risk of injury. Nothing will suffice short of an agreement to waive any claim for negligence. The plaintiff must agree either expressly or impliedly, to waive any claim for injury that may befall him due to the lack of reasonable care by the defendant, or more accurately, due to the failure of the defendant to measure up to the standard of care that the law requires of him."

In *Nettleship* the claimant had agreed to take the defendant out for a driving lesson. The claimant was injured as a result of the defendant's negligent driving. The claimant was held not to have been *volenti* since he had asked for, and had been given, an assurance by the defendant that she had insurance cover. The consent must be to the particular risk which is involved in the accident: *Gilmore* v *London CC* (1938). For example, in *Gleghorn* v *Oldham* (1927) a caddie was injured by a golfer who was demonstrating a shot. It was held that the simple fact of the claimant going on to the course did not mean that he had thereby assumed the risk of injury by the defendant's negligence.

The defence of *volenti* can never apply so as to license (or to waive potential liability) in advance of a subsequent act of negligence, since the pursuer would not have full knowledge of the extent, as well as the nature, of the duty of care which was owed to him: *Dann* v *Hamilton* (1939). See also *Titchener* v *BRB* (1984).

The defence of *volenti* is unlikely to succeed in an employer–employee situation (for example, the employee has been injured on account of his employer's negligence) since it will be assumed that the pursuer (the employee) is not truly *volenti*, in that he is working under economic pressure: *Bowater* v *Rowley Regis Corp* (1944); *Smith* v *Baker and Sons* (1891).

The defence is also unlikely to succeed in relation to the injury which is sustained by someone who is attempting to perform a rescue. The leading case on this point is *Baker* v *T E Hopkins and Son Ltd* (1959). In that case, the defendant company was involved in cleaning a well. In order to do so, a petrol-driven pump was used. The defendant's negligence led to the well becoming filled with carbon monoxide gas. Two employees were overcome with the fumes and collapsed. A doctor was called to the scene. He was informed that there were two men who had collapsed down the well. The doctor was advised not to go down the well for his own safety. However, he decided to do so. He was lowered into the well but found that the workers had died. He asked to be lifted to the surface, but when he was being raised the rope lifting him became caught. He could not be raised further and he died. It was held that the defence of *volenti non fit iniuria* was inapplicable. However, the defence will succeed if the rescue attempt is foolhardy: *Sylvester* v *Chapman Ltd* (1935). In that case the claimant was mauled by a leopard when he crossed a barrier in front of the leopard's cage in order to put out a cigarette smouldering in the straw. It was held that the claimant was not attempting to save life or property, as there were other people in the vicinity who could have extinguished the fire without being mauled.

## ILLEGALITY

The gist of this defence is that the law will not allow the pursuer to succeed in a delictual action, if at the time, he was injured he was engaged in an illegal activity. This principle is expressed in the Latin maxim *ex turpi causa non oritur actio*. Let us consider the following two scenarios.

First, John runs an off-licence. Five minutes after he can legally sell alcohol, and just as he is about to close his shop to the public, Robert, a regular customer, comes into the shop to purchase a crate of beer. John sells Robert the beer. As John is accompanying Robert to the door, he negligently drops the crate on John's foot, which is broken. If John were to sue Robert in negligence, could the latter invoke the defence of illegality to the effect that John was performing (or had just performed) an illegal act when the accident occurred?

Second, Brian decides to stage an armed robbery of a post office. While he is making his "getaway" he trips on a hole in the carpet at the front door. He is injured as a consequence. Would the defence of illegality be applicable here?

The defence of illegality would almost certainly be applicable in the second scenario, but not in the first, on the basis that it is only the more socially reprehensible illegal acts that carry the defence. The defence represents a grey area of the law. It is, therefore, difficult to predict with certainty whether a court will allow it to succeed.

There is an overlap of the defence of illegality with the defences of contributory negligence and also consent (*volenti*) which have already been discussed. In the Court of Appeal case of *Murphy* v *Culhane* (1977) the defendant had pleaded guilty to the manslaughter of the claimant's husband. It was held that the defendant could raise all three defences because the deceased had initiated the affray with the defendant.

The defence is probably limited to criminal activity on the part of the pursuer. In *Reeves* v *Metropolitan Police Commissioner* (1999) the husband of the claimant committed suicide while in police custody. The defendants had failed to take the necessary precautions to ensure his safety. The Court of Appeal held that the defence of *ex turpi causa* did not apply. Although the decision of the court on this defence could have been clearer, one factor which influenced it was that suicide is no longer a criminal offence. See also *Kirkham* v *Chief Constable of Greater Manchester Police* (1990).

In the Court of Appeal case of *Pitts* v *Hunt* (1991) both the claimant and the defendant had been drinking heavily prior to embarking on a motorcycle ride. The claimant, who was a pillion passenger, encouraged the defendant, who did not have a driving licence, to ride in a dangerous and reckless manner. The cycle was involved in an accident. The claimant was seriously injured and the defendant was killed. It was held that the defence of illegality precluded the claimant from recovering from the estate of the deceased. One of the reasons which influenced the court was that in a joint illegal enterprise of this kind it was difficult to ascertain the appropriate standard of care which one demands of the defendant. Therefore, no duty of care is owed by the defendant to the claimant in law. The recent case of *Beaumont* v *Ferrer* (2014) illustrates the application of the defence. In that case, the claimant conspired, with other youths, to book a taxi but "jump the taxi", that is, hastily exit the taxi without paying. As the taxi approached its destination, several youths managed to exit the taxi and run away. Realising that the youths had no intention of paying him, the defendant drove off, with the claimant still in the taxi. The response by the claimant was to jump out of the taxi. He was seriously injured as a consequence. He raised an action against the defendant, claiming that the latter owed him a duty of care and that such a duty had been breached. The defendant successfully invoked the defence of *ex turpi causa non oritur actio*, or illegality.

Sometimes the courts simply say that it is against public policy to hold that a duty of care is owed between those who are involved in a joint criminal enterprise. This point is well illustrated in *Ashton* v *Turner* (1981). In that case, the claimant and the defendant were making a "getaway" in a car which was being driven by the defendant, after committing a burglary. The car was involved in an accident because the defendant and claimant had been heavily drinking. It was held that this was a "no-duty" situation. No duty of care was owed by the defendant to the claimant.

In ascertaining whether the defence of illegality applies, the court takes into account the degree of moral turpitude which is associated with the pursuer's conduct. For example, in *Weir* v *Wyper* (1992) the pursuer, a girl aged 16, asked the defender (who the former knew possessed only a provisional driving licence) to drive her home. The defender drove negligently and the pursuer was injured. She sued the defender. It was held in the Outer House that the defence of illegality did not apply. Each case had to be decided on its own facts. In contrast, in *Duncan* v *Ross Harper and Murphy* (1993) the pursuer, a 19-year-old man, was injured while a passenger in a car which was being negligently driven by the defendant. The car had been stolen and the pursuer had been involved in the theft. He sued his solicitors for failing to raise an action on his behalf timeously. It was held that since the defence of illegality could have been successfully invoked by the negligent driver, the pursuer failed in his action against the solicitor. *Revill* v *Newbury* (1996) is authority for the proposition that the defence of illegality is less likely to succeed if the harm, which is the subject-matter of the action, has been intentionally inflicted on the pursuer. In *Revill* the claimant was shot and injured by the defendant while the former was raiding the defendant's allotment. It was held that the defence of illegality was inapplicable.

A recent example of the courts taking into account the degree of moral turpitude which is associated with the act of the pursuer, is illustrated in *Buckett* v *Staffordshire CC* (2015) In that case, the claimant, who was aged 16 at the time the accident took place, was trespassing on the roof of a school building one weekend. In the course of so doing, he fell through a fragile area of glass which was part of a skylight. He sustained serious injuries as a result of his fall. He sued the defendant, claiming that as occupier of the school, the defendant had breached its statutory duty to him. In turn, the defendant invoked the defence of illegality, asserting that, up to the time of his fall, the claimant, with others, was engaged in a course of conduct which the former alleged to have amounted, *inter alia*, to wanton vandalism, and criminal damage. In rejecting the defence, Judge Main QC expressed the opinion that if the claimant had fallen through the skylight while committing criminal damage to the skylight, the defence would have been successful. However, at the time the accident took place, the claimant had ceased engaging in any acts of criminal damage and dishonesty. He was merely trespassing on the school roof. In the last analysis, the tort of trespass failed to offend any public interest.

Finally, there must be a direct causal link between the harm which the pursuer sustains and the illegal act, in relation to which the defence of illegality is invoked. This point is illustrated in both *Beaumont* v *Ferrer* and *Buckett* v *Staffordshire CC* which we have already discussed. Whereas in *Beaumont* the claimant's illegal conduct was inextricably connected with the harm which he sustained and which was the cause of the action, in *Buckett* the claimant had ceased his acts of criminal damage etc when the accident which injured him took place. In the last analysis, there was no causal link between those acts and the harm which he later sustained.

## STATUTORY AUTHORITY

The pursuer cannot successfully sue the defender if statute has authorised the harm which is complained of: *X* v *Bedfordshire County Council* (1995).

The defence is most commonly invoked in relation to the law of nuisance. In *Metropolitan Asylum District* v *Hill* (1880–81) a local authority defendant was authorised by statute to erect a hospital for infectious disease. The statute provided that the defendant could erect hospitals of such a size and according to such a plan, as it considered fit. A hospital was built near the claimant's house. He raised an action in nuisance. The House of Lords held that the local authority had no statutory authority to commit the nuisance in question, since the hospital could have been erected in such a location as not to cause a nuisance. However, the defence of statutory authority does not apply if the defender has acted negligently: *Geddis* v *Proprietors of Bann Reservoir* (1887–88).

The leading case on the defence of statutory authority is now the House of Lords case of *Allen* v *Gulf Oil Refining Ltd* (1981). In that case, a private Act of Parliament authorised the construction of an oil refinery. After the refinery started operating, there were complaints about smell and noise which emanated from the plant. An action in nuisance was raised against the defendants. However, it was held that since the inevitable consequence of that which was authorised was the creation of a nuisance, the defence of statutory authority applied.

## DAMNUM FATALE

The defence of *damnum fatale* or, as it is sometimes known, an Act of God or *vis maior*, is very rarely invoked in Scots law. There is little modern authority on this defence. The relevant occurrence must arise from natural causes, without human intervention, and must go beyond anything which is reasonably foreseeable or preventable. A natural event will not rank as a *damnum fatale* simply because it rarely happens. For example, in *Caledonian Railway Company* v *Greenock Corporation* (1917) the Corporation altered the channel of a burn. During an exceptionally heavy rainfall, the burn overflowed and damaged property which belonged to the pursuer. The burn, in its natural state, would have carried away the water effectively. The defender argued that the heavy rainfall ranked as a *damnum fatale*. However, the House of Lords rejected this defence.

## INEVITABLE ACCIDENT

The defence of inevitable accident applies when an occurrence which could not have been reasonably avoided, occurs. In *Ryan* v *Youngs* (1938) the defendants employed a man to drive a lorry. He was ostensibly in good health but, in fact, he suffered from fatty degeneration of the heart. One day, he suddenly died at the wheel of his lorry. The vehicle went out of control, mounted the kerb, and injured the claimant. It transpired that the lorry driver's death was caused by his medical condition. The Court of Appeal held that the defence of inevitable accident applied.

## NECESSITY

The defence of necessity is applicable only in cases of emergency. It is a defence on which there is little modern authority. The action which is taken by the defender who invokes the defence, must be reasonable or proportionate to the danger which he is attempting to counter. In *Cope* v *Sharpe (No 2)* (1912) the defendant trespassed on the claimant's land in order to prevent fire spreading to land over which his master had shooting rights. It was held that the defence of necessity was applicable.

## *RES IUDICATA*

The defence of *res iudicata* is to the effect that the issue which is before the court, has already been litigated between the same parties, and has been determined by a competent court. A plea of *res iudicata* will succeed if there is identity as to:

(a) the parties;

(b) the subject-matter of the dispute; and

(c) the *media concludendi*, that is to say, that the first and second suit must present one, and the same, ground of action.

In *Matuszczyk* v *NCB* (1955) a miner raised an action against the National Coal Board, claiming that the Board had failed to provide a safe system of work and that a shot firer had breached various common-law duties. The defenders were absolved of liability and the pursuer failed in his action. The miner proceeded to raise a second action for the same injuries. This time, he based his case on a breach of statutory duty. It was held, however, that the question which fell to be answered in the latter case was precisely that which had been answered in the first, namely whether the accident had been caused by the fault of the defender. Therefore, the defence of *res iudicata* was successfully invoked.

## Essential Facts

- The court can reduce damages which are awarded to the pursuer if he has been contributorily negligent.
- Damages are reduced to the extent which the court considers is just and equitable.
- It is essential that the pursuer's conduct contributes to the damage which he sustains for the defence to apply.
- The standard of care which applies to the defence of contributory negligence is the same as that which applies generally in the law of negligence.
- Where a person consents to run the risk of injury he cannot thereafter claim damages for the injury which was caused by the risk.
- The defence operates as a complete defence.
- For the defence to apply the defender requires to prove that the pursuer, with full knowledge of the nature and extent of the risk which he ran, freely and voluntarily agreed to incur it.
- The defence of *volenti* can never apply so as to license or to waive potential liability in advance of a subsequent act of negligence.
- The defence is unlikely to succeed in an employer–employee situation.
- The law will not allow the pursuer to recover if he was involved in an illegal activity when the accident occurred.
- The defence of illegality operates as a complete defence.
- The defence is probably limited to criminal activity on the part of the pursuer.
- In ascertaining whether the defence applies, the court takes into account the degree of moral turpitude which is associated with the pursuer's conduct.
- The pursuer cannot raise an action in relation to that which Parliament has authorised.
- The defence of *damnum fatale* is rarely invoked in Scots law.
- The relevant event must arise from natural causes without human intervention and must go beyond anything which is reasonably foreseeable or preventable.
- A natural event will not rank as a *damnum fatale* simply because it rarely happens.

- The defence of inevitable accident applies when an accident which could not have been reasonably avoided, occurs.
- The defence of necessity is applicable only in cases of emergency.
- The action which is taken by the defender must be reasonable, or proportionate, in relation to the danger which he is attempting to counter.
- The defence of *res iudicata* is to the effect that the issue which is before the court has already been litigated between the parties and has been determined by a competent court. A plea of *res iudicata* will succeed if there is identity as to the parties, the subject-matter of the dispute and the *media concludendi* (that is to say that the first and second suit must present one and the same ground of action).

## Essential Cases

**Quintas v National Smelting Co (1961)**: in relation to the defence of contributory negligence, the sum which falls to be deducted from the damages which are awarded to the pursuer depends on the respective responsibilities of the parties and "what is just and equitable, having regard thereto can only be assessed when it has been found what the claimant in fact did and what the defendants failed in their duty to do".

**Froom v Butcher (1976)**: essential that the pursuer's conduct contributes to the damage which the pursuer sustains in order for the defence of contributory negligence to apply.

**Jones v Livox Quarries Ltd (1952)**: for the defence to apply, the pursuer requires to be able to foresee the risk of injury to himself and his failing to take the relevant prophylactic action.

**Nettleship v Weston (1971)**: the claimant agreed to take the defendant out for a driving lesson. The former was injured by virtue of the defendant's negligent driving. The claimant was held not to have been *volenti* since he had asked for and had been given an assurance by the defendant that she had insurance cover.

**Pitts v Hunt (1991)**: both the claimant and the defendant had been heavily drinking prior to embarking on a motorcycle ride. The plaintiff, who was a pillion passenger, encouraged the defendant, who did not have a driving licence, to ride in a dangerous and reckless manner. The cycle was involved in an accident. The claimant was seriously injured and the defendant was killed. Held that the defence of illegality applied.

**Allen v Gulf Oil Refining Ltd (1981)**: a private Act of Parliament authorised the construction of an oil refinery. After the refinery started operating, there were complaints about smell and noise from the plant. It was held that since the inevitable consequence of that which was authorised was the creation of the nuisance, the defence of statutory authority applied.

**Caledonian Railway Co v Greenock Corporation (1917)**: a natural event will not rank as a *damnum fatale* simply because it rarely happens. The Corporation altered the channel of a burn. During an exceptionally heavy rainfall the burn overflowed and damaged property which belonged to the pursuer. The defender argued that the heavy rainfall ranked as a *damnum fatale*. The House of Lords rejected this defence.

**Ryan v Youngs (1938)**: the defendants employed a man to drive a lorry. He was ostensibly in good health but, in fact, he suffered from fatty degeneration of the heart. One day he suddenly died at the wheel of his lorry and he injured the claimant. It was held that the defence of inevitable accident applied.

**Cope v Sharpe (1912)**: the defendant trespassed on the claimant's land in order to prevent fire spreading to land over which his master had shooting rights. It was held that the defence of necessity was applicable.

**Matuszczyk v NCB (1955)**: a miner raised an action against the National Coal Board, claiming that the Board had failed to provide a safe system of work and that a shot firer had breached various common-law duties. The defenders were absolved of liability and the pursuer failed in his action. The miner proceeded to raise a second action for the same injuries. This time he based his case on a breach of statutory duty. It was held that the question which fell to be answered in the latter case was precisely that which was answered in the first, namely, whether the accident had been caused by the fault of the defender. The defence of *res iudicata* was therefore successfully invoked.

# 12 REMEDIES

The main remedies, as far as the law of delict is concerned, namely interdict, damages and declarator, are now discussed.

## INTERDICT

In *Hay's Trustees* v *Young* (1877) Lord Gifford stated that interdict is a remedy which proceeds on the principle that prevention is better than cure, and that in many cases, it is more expedient to prevent a wrong from being done, than simply to attempt to give redress after that wrong occurs. In *Kelso School Board* v *Hunter* (1874) Lord Deas stated that an interdict was an extraordinary remedy, not to be given except for urgent reasons, and even then, not as a matter of right, but only in the exercise of a sound judicial discretion.

Interdict is an appropriate remedy to prevent an existing wrong from continuing or to prevent a wrong from being done in the future, where there are reasonable grounds for apprehending that a wrong is intended to be committed: *Inverurie Magistrates* v *Sorrie* (1956). An interdict is not appropriate where a wrong has been completed and there is no threat of repetition: *Associated Displays Ltd (in liquidation)* v *Turnbeam Ltd* (1988); and *Crooke* v *Scots Pictorial Publishing Co Ltd* (1906).

An interdict may be perpetual, applying without limit of time, or it may be interim, and therefore designed to preserve the *status quo* in order to prevent an impending wrong. An interim interdict may be sought at any stage of a process for permanent interdict, either alone, or with other legal remedies such as judicial review, declarator or damages: Scott-Robinson, *The Law of Interdict* (2nd edn, 1994) p 2.

The process of interdict is quasi-criminal, that is to say, if the party who is interdicted fails to comply with the terms of the interdict, he is liable to summary punishment, fine or imprisonment and may be found liable in expenses: *McIntyre* v *Sheridan* (1993). The terms of the interdict must be precise: *Webster* v *Lord Advocate* (1985). Furthermore, the terms of the interdict must be also be no wider than that necessary to abate the nuisance in question.

The interdict is a purely personal remedy, that is to say, an interdict is directed against the person who is named in the action. An existing owner of premises cannot, therefore, be interdicted in respect of a nuisance which has been committed by a previous owner.

In order to succeed in an action for interdict, the pursuer must establish that some legal right or interest of his is being infringed. In other words, the pursuer must have title and interest to sue: *D and J Nicol* v *Dundee Harbour Trustees* (1915). An interdict is not available where the law provides for an alternative remedy: *Johnston* v *Thomson* (1877). Furthermore, the application for interdict must be timeous or prompt. In *Lowson's Trustees* v *Crammond* (1964) an application for an interdict to prevent the erection of buildings was refused, since the buildings, which were the subject-matter of the action, were just about to be completed.

Simply because the subject matter of the proceedings has social utility or value does not preclude an interdict from being granted: *Webster* v *Lord Advocate* (1984).

The court has no jurisdiction to grant interdict against the Crown, or against any of its officers, where the result would be to grant relief against the Crown: Crown Proceedings Act 1947, ss 21(2) and 43(a). See, however, *R* v *Secretary of State for Transport, ex parte Factortame (No 2)* (1991) where the European Court of Justice held that if a national court decided that the only obstacle which precluded it from granting an interim injunction (which is the English equivalent of interdict) was a national rule of law, that rule had to be set aside.

## DECLARATOR

A declarator is a judicial remedy whereby the court simply makes a statement of the pursuer's legal rights, for example, that a particular adverse state of affairs ranks as a nuisance in law: *Webster* v *Lord Advocate*. The declarator does not order the defender to do anything. The court will only grant a declarator in relation to a matter which constitutes a live and practical issue between the parties concerned, in contrast to something which is purely academic or hypothetical: *Macnaughten* v *Macnaughten* (1953).

A declarator may be sought with other remedies such as interdict: *Webster* v *Lord Advocate* and *Edinburgh and District Water Trustees* v *Clippens Oil Co Ltd* (1889).

## DAMAGES

The award of damages is the normal form of remedy for a delictual wrong. "Money is the universal solvent. Everything can be turned into money that is either a gain or a loss. Money is asked and damages are due for reparation of every possible suffering or injury": *Auld* v *Shairp* (1874). The purpose of the award of damages is to effect *restitutio in integrum*, that is, to restore the pursuer as far as possible to the position he was in before the relevant delictual conduct took place: Stair, 1.9.2.

The law of delict in Scotland is not concerned with punishing the wrongdoer. Rather, it is about compensating the victim: *Gibson* v *Anderson* (1846). However, in relation to damages for personal injury, it is unrealistic to talk of *restitutio in integrum*. Can one really be restored to one's original position in relation to a lost limb? It is more realistic, therefore, in such circumstances, to describe the damages which the court awards as "compensation".

The amount of damages which the court awards bears no relationship to the degree of fault on the part of the defender.

## Damage to property

Where property has been damaged, the pursuer is entitled to the cost of repair of damage to the property. In relation to damages for the total loss of corporeal property, the court calculates damages based on the market value of the property concerned. For example, in *Hutchison* v *Davidson* (1945) a house was burned to the ground. The Inner House held that damages should be based on the difference between market values, before and after, the fire which destroyed the premises. *Hutchison* concerned heritable property. However, the same principle applies to moveable property: *The Susquehanna* (1926).

The pursuer is also entitled to recover economic loss which derives from the damage in question. However, economic loss which derives from the impecuniousity of the pursuer is normally not recoverable: *Liesbosch Dredger* v *SS Edison* (1933). But the courts have never felt particularly comfortable about this decision, and have proceeded to award damages to compensate loss which directly derives from the impecuniousity of the pursuer: *McIver* v *Judge* (1994).

It should be remembered here that, generally speaking, one cannot recover for pure economic loss in the law of delict: *McFarlane* v *Tayside Health Board* (2000).

## Damages for personal injury

The pursuer is entitled to reparation in respect of his personal injury and any derivative economic loss. However, *no* monetary sum can really compensate the pursuer for physical injury: see, for example, *Admiralty Commissioners* v *SS Valeria* (1922).

## Solatium

An award of damages for *solatium* represents compensation for the pain and suffering the pursuer has suffered as a result of the defender's conduct. Where pain and injury will continue after the date of proof, the *solatium* award will be apportioned between past and future *solatium*. In making a *solatium* award the court takes into account the gravity and extent of the relevant injury; the pursuer's awareness of any pain; the pain and suffering which has been already experienced; future pain and suffering; loss of amenity (ie enjoyment of life); and the impact on the pursuer of his awareness that his life expectancy has been diminished.

### Patrimonial loss

Patrimonial loss covers all pecuniary or financial loss which is sustained by the pursuer. The court takes into account both past and future pecuniary loss. Past patrimonial loss covers losses sustained between the date of the delictual act and the date of the proof, whereas future patrimonial loss relates to losses which the pursuer will suffer subsequent to the proof. The latter loss is of particular relevance in relation to severe injury. Generally speaking, the younger the pursuer is the more matters which require to be taken into account when calculating patrimonial loss, such as loss of career promotion opportunities.

As far as the loss of *past* earnings is concerned, the pursuer's net income requires to be established. This is done by deducting tax, national insurance contributions and pension contributions In order to assess future loss of earnings the court must establish the net annual earnings of the pursuer as at the date of proof: *McGarrigle v Babcock Energy Ltd* (1996). This is known as the *multiplicand*. One then finds the *multiplier*. This is determined by taking into account the pursuer's age and probable retirement age. The multiplier is usually less than the remaining number of years which the pursuer has to work, since one must take into account uncertainties, such as the possibility of redundancy, death, accidents etc. Once the multiplier and the multiplicand have been established they are simply multiplied together in order to give a lump sum. However, if the pursuer is able to work in some capacity after the accident, the court is required to establish the difference between likely future earnings which the pursuer would have earned had the pursuer not been disabled (the multiplicand) and then apply the appropriate multiplier: *Stark v Lothian and Borders Fire Board* (1993).

In some cases, the court will not employ the multiplicand/multiplier method of calculating future patrimonial loss. For example, where the pursuer has been able to continue working, albeit on lighter work than formerly, or where there is evidence that the pursuer will be able to continue working in a lower paid job than previously: *Stevenson* v *British Coal Board* (1989).

Interest is payable on damages under the Interest on Damages (Scotland) Act 1958, as amended by the Interest on Damages (Scotland) Act 1971.

Loss of pension rights are also taken into account (*Barratt* v *Strathclyde Fire Brigade* (1984)), as are outlays and expenses. For example, damages can be recovered in respect of maintenance costs (*McMillan* v *McDowell* (1993)); reasonable medical expenses (*Lewis* v *Laird Line* (1925)); nursing costs (*McIntosh* v *NCB* (1988)). It is irrelevant if similar treatment is available on the NHS: Law Reform (Personal Injuries) Act 1948, s 2(4). Both past and future outlays require to be taken into account.

Sometimes when someone is injured that person may seek compensation:

(a) in relation to services which are rendered to him *by* his relatives as a result of such injuries; and/or

(b) services which, owing to his injuries he is no longer able to render *to* his relatives.

As far as "(a)" is concerned, s 8(1) of the Administration of Justice Act 1982 provides that where necessary services have been rendered to the injured person by a relative (as defined in s 13, as amended) then unless the relative has expressly agreed – in the knowledge that an action for damages has been raised or is in contemplation – that no payment should be made in respect of those services, the responsible person is liable to pay the injured person, by way of damages, such sum as represents reasonable remuneration for those services, and reasonable expenses which are incurred in connection therewith. The relative has no right of action against the wrongdoer: s 8(4). Under the Law Reform (Miscellaneous Provisions) (Scotland) Act 1990 (which amends the 1982 Act), s 8(3) of the latter now permits recovery of the cost of necessary services which are rendered by a relative after the date of an award of damages. The injured party is under a duty to account to the relative for past services, but not for future services.

As far as "(b)" is concerned, this head is of special importance for housewives. If the pursuer has died, the relative can claim under s 6(1) of the Damages (Scotland) Act 2011. If the pursuer is still alive, only the pursuer can claim: s 9(4) Administration of Justice Act 1982.

The quantification of damages is more difficult and speculative in relation to children. The court will usually consider how the child is performing at school and his intelligence etc.

Under the Social Security (Recovery of Benefits) Act 1997 the Government can recover certain state benefits which have been paid in relation to an accident etc, where the person claiming the benefits also receives compensation from a third party. This prevents the injured person from being compensated twice for the same injury. Recoupable benefits include income support, disability benefits, mobility allowance and attendance allowance.

## Damages where the pursuer has died

It may sometimes happen that the pursuer, who has sustained harm which has been caused by the defender, dies before the relevant trial. Under the Damages (Scotland) Act 2011 a claim for *solatium* up to the date of death of the injured party transmits to the executor in the same way as patrimonial loss: s 2. The death of the injured party need not have been caused by the defender.

Section 4 of the 2011 Act allows a non-patrimonial award to be made for loss which used to be referred to as a "loss of society" award. The non-patrimonial loss award can only be claimed by the immediate family of the deceased, which includes a spouse or cohabitee (including civil partner), a parent, a child or someone who has been accepted by the deceased, as a child of the family. The non-patrimonial award, which the immediate family can claim, provides for compensation in respect of distress and anxiety endured in contemplation of the deceased before death, grief and sorrow caused by the deceased's death, and loss of such non-patrimonial benefit as the immediate family member might have expected from the deceased's society and guidance if the deceased had not died.

It often happens that the deceased may have financially supported relatives prior to his death. Section 4 of the 2011 Act allows a wider group of individuals (than those who can sue for a non-patrimonial loss award) to claim for such loss. Section 7 fixes the total amount to be available to support relatives of the deceased, to an amount equivalent to 75 per cent of the deceased's net income.

Usually, damages are awarded on "once and for all" basis. That is to say, all losses which derive from a delictual act must be recovered in one action by the pursuer. However, such a way of compensating victims may not always secure a fair result. For example, I may sustain serious injury at work as a result of the negligence of my employer, the upshot of which is that, notwithstanding the fact that I can currently continue working, the nature of my injury is such that in the future, my physical condition will seriously deteriorate to the extent that I will be rendered almost immobile. Under s 12 of the Administration of Justice Act 1982 the court can make an award of provisional damages in relation to personal injuries. Such an award can be made only when it is either proved, or admitted, that at some definite or indefinite time in the future, the injured person will either develop some serious disease or suffer some serious deterioration in his physical or mental condition. Furthermore, provisional damages can be awarded only if the defender was, at the time of the accident, either a public authority or an insured person. Finally, if the court decides to award provisional damages to the pursuer, the nature of the deterioration on the occurrence of which the pursuer's right to final damages will emerge, must be made clear to both parties: *Bonar v Trafalgar House Offshore Fabrication Ltd* (1996).

## PRESCRIPTION AND LIMITATION

### Prescription

Under s 6 of the Prescription and Limitation (Scotland) Act 1973 (PLSA) the obligation to make reparation for a delictual act is extinguished after 5 years. The relevant period runs from the date on which the delict is complete. Time begins to run when the pursuer became aware or could, with reasonable diligence, have become aware of the harm in question: s 11(3). There must be a concurrence of *damnum* and *iniuria* before the prescriptive period can commence to run. Delictual liability, in relation to personal injury and death, no longer prescribes: ss 6(2) and 7(2).

Some obligations are subject to what is known as long negative prescription, and become prescribed only after a period of 20 years: s 7(1). An example of such long negative prescription would be an action for interdict for a nuisance which has been in existence for more than 20 years. However, an action for damages in relation to a nuisance which injures my property, and in relation to which I demand compensation from the defender, would prescribe after 5 years.

### Limitation

Whereas claims for death and personal injury are imprescribable, such claims are subject to the rules on limitation. A claim for reparation in respect of death and personal injury must be brought within 3 years of the relevant injury or death: ss 17 and 18. As far as claims for personal injury are concerned, the relevant date begins to run from the date on which the injury was sustained, or the act or omission ceased, whichever is the later. One takes into account the date on which either the pursuer became aware, or it would have been reasonably practicable for him to become aware, that his injuries are sufficiently serious to justify proceedings, and that they were attributable to an act or omission of the defender. As far as a child is concerned, the relevant action must be raised within 3 years of the child attaining the age of 16: Age of Legal Capacity (Scotland) Act 1991, s 1.

Finally, the court has power to allow an action to proceed outwith the 3-year period if it deems it equitable to do so: PLSA, s 19A.

## Essential Facts

- The interdict prevents an existing wrong from continuing or prevents a wrong from being done in the future.
- An interdict may be perpetual or interim.
- The pursuer must establish that some legal right or interest of his is being infringed.
- A declarator is a judicial remedy where the court simply makes a statement of the pursuer's legal rights.
- The award of damages is the normal remedy for a delictual wrong. The purpose of damages is to restore the pursuer, as far as possible, to the position he was in before the relevant delictual act took place.
- Where property has been damaged the pursuer is entitled to the cost of repair of damage to the property.
- The pursuer is also entitled to recover economic loss which derives from the damage in question.
- As far as damages for personal injury are concerned, the pursuer is entitled to reparation for injury to his person and any derivative economic loss.
- Where pain and injury will continue after the date of proof, the *solatium* award will be apportioned between past and future *solatium*.
- The court takes into account past and future pecuniary loss.
- The pursuer can recover in relation to services rendered to him by his relatives as a result of the accident and services which he is no longer able to render to his relatives.
- The obligation to make reparation for a delictual act is extinguished after 5 years. Claims for death and personal injury are subject to the rules on limitation and must be brought within 3 years of the relevant injury or death.

# INDEX